It's a rare how-to book on parenting that doesn't leave you feeling buried under a disheartenin̲̅g̲̅ .... ̲̅rden of guilt. In *Opening Your Child's* .... Fuller does a warm and masterful jo .... nd sea- soned insight in a parent-to .... ̲̅es you with the feeling you really ca ....

This is a smart, highly readable, and inspiring look at how we can raise our kids to realize all of the wondrous potential God has blessed them with. This book will help you see and set free the mir- acle that's hiding behind that grape-jelly grin at your house.

DAVID KOPP
SENIOR EDITOR
Christian Parenting Today

We've known for a long time about the importance of a child's early experiences in determining whether that child achieves his or her God-given potential to learn, to think, and to move. In *Opening Your Child's Nine Learning Windows*, Cheri Fuller provides parents with a clear road map for those critical early years, by detailing the sim- ple things they can do to enhance their child's learning potential. She also gives "learning window closers" parents should avoid. *Opening Your Child's Nine Learning Windows* is a "must read" for every parent who wants to optimize their child's outcome.

MARIANNE NEIFERT, M.D.
AUTHOR OF
Dr. Mom: A Guide to Baby and Child Care
and *Dr. Mom's Prescription for Preschoolers*

Also by Cheri Fuller

Opening Your Child's Spiritual Windows
When Children Pray
When Mothers Pray
Extraordinary Kids: Nurturing and Championing Your Child
with Special Needs
Quiet Whispers from God's Heart for Women
21 Days to Helping Your Child Learn
Teaching Your Child to Write
Trading Your Worry for Wonder
Christmas Treasures of the Heart
Unlocking Your Child's Learning Potential
365 Ways to Develop Values in Your Child
365 Ways to Build Your Child's Self-Esteem
365 Ways to Help Your Child Learn and Achieve
How to Grow a Young Music Lover
Home Business Happiness
Helping Your Child Succeed in Public School
Motivating Your Kids from Crayons to Career
Home-Life: The Key to Your Child's Success at School

cheri fuller

opening your child's nine *learning* windows

Formerly titled
Through the Learning Glass

ZONDERVAN™

GRAND RAPIDS, MICHIGAN 49530

We want to hear from you. Please send your comments about this book
to us in care of the address below. Thank you.

GRAND RAPIDS, MICHIGAN 49530
www.zondervan.com

ZONDERVAN™

Opening Your Child's Nine Learning Windows
Copyright © 1999 by Cheri Fuller
Formerly titled *Through the Learning Glass*

Requests for information should be addressed to:

Zondervan, *Grand Rapids, Michigan 49530*

Library of Congress Cataloging-in-Publication Data

Fuller, Cheri.
      Opening your child's nine learning windows / Cheri Fuller.
         p. cm.
      Rev. ed. of: Through the learning glass. ©1999.
      Includes bibliographical references.
      ISBN 0-310-23994-X (softcover)
      1. Learning. 2. Education—Parent participation. I. Fuller, Cheri. Through the
learning glass. II. Title.
LB1060.F85 2001
370.15'23—dc21   00-068053
                                                                                CIP

Published in association with the literary agency of Alive Communications, Inc., 7680
Goddard Street, Suite 200, Colorado Springs, CO 80920.

Interior design by Sherri L. Hoffman

Printed in the United States of America

---

01 02 03 04 05 /❖ DC/ 10 9 8 7 6 5 4 3 2

To Caitlin Elizabeth Fuller and all the children who wonder and dance, question and create, blow bubbles, sing songs, and make life wonderful for us parents and grandparents

contents

acknowledgments

My sincere thanks to those who contributed insights, support, and prayers for this project, including family and adolescent psychologist Dr. Ken Wilgus for his review of the Emotions Window chapter; pediatric physical therapist Kay Davis for consulting on and reviewing the Physical Window chapter; neurosurgeon Dr. Richard V. Smith for his input and review of chapter 1, The Learning Windows; Sally Wilgus; Suzee Feree; Linda Merrick; Julie Hockensmith; Mary Manz Simon; Ellen Stewart; and Connie Baker.

I'm grateful to my children, Justin, Christopher, and Alison, because you've not only brought so much joy into our lives but also for what you taught me in your growing-up years. You've provided much inspiration for this book. And for Caitlin, our granddaughter, whose wonderful growth and development in her first year of life has filled us with much gratitude to God and provided several anecdotes for this book.

And to all the parents like Joy Griffin, Melissa King, Tiffany Fuller, and others who were willing to share incidents from the Learning Windows of their children, thanks!

The support and encouragement from my husband, Holmes, is quiet, steady, and full of love, for this project and everything else I do, and I'm grateful.

I appreciate how graciously Greg Johnson has represented me, for the skillful editing of Sandy Vander Zicht and Jane Haradine, and the privilege of working with the professional staff at Zondervan Publishing House.

My thanks to Ellen Stewart, a music therapist, who reviewed and consulted the Music Window chapter.

I am constantly amazed at the way children learn and grow, at the incredible potential within them, at the learning windows of opportunity we have in the fleeting years of childhood—and have no one to thank for that but God, our heavenly Father and Creator! For us as parents and for our children, he can provide the ultimate motivation to live and love, to grow and become all we are meant to be.

One

the learning windows

Children are a gift from the Lord;
they are a reward from him.

PSALM 127:3 NLT

Three-year-old Michael was so excited about the prospect of a new baby sister that he started to sing to her even before she was born. He and his mother, Karen, made his singing part of their daily routine.

One day Karen noticed something strange. Depending on what song Michael was singing, the baby either began kicking or, with a change of tune, became unusually still, as if sleeping. After a while, Karen could almost predict how her unborn daughter would react to Michael's songs.

The pregnancy progressed normally and the family waited expectantly for the new arrival. But when Karen's labor began, complications developed. Everyone in the delivery room knew that the baby was in trouble. When she was finally born, her skin was a dusky bluish red, and her breathing was erratic. In "critical condition," the baby was rushed to a nearby neonatal intensive care unit.

The tiny infant's condition, instead of improving, became worse each day. Finally the pediatrician told the parents that there was little hope and they should prepare for the worst. The doctor did not expect the baby to survive. Instead of looking forward to a joyous homecoming with family and friends, they planned the baby's funeral. They told Michael.

Distraught, Michael begged to be able to see his baby sister. "I want to sing to her!" he pleaded. "Please!"

Karen realized that if Michael didn't see his sister soon, it would be too late.

Despite strict rules barring children from the Neonatal Intensive Care Unit, Karen dressed Michael in an adult-size hospital scrub suit and together they walked into the NICU. The head nurse immediately ordered him out.

But Karen wouldn't budge. "He's not leaving until he sings to his sister!" Still holding Michael's hand, she walked over to stand beside her daughter. Karen could hear every breath as the tiny infant struggled for life. Michael looked intently at the tiny sister. After a few minutes he took a deep breath and began to sing. "'You are my sunshine, my only sunshine. You make me happy when skies are gray....'"

The infant seemed to respond. Her pulse rate began to calm down.

"Keep singing, Michael!" Karen urged.

"'You'll never know, dear, how much I love you, please don't take my sunshine away.'"

The baby's ragged, labored breathing eased. She was no longer having to fight so hard for each breath.

"Don't stop, Michael," Karen said, her voice just above a whisper as she watched this miraculous change in her baby.

"'The other night, dear, as I lay sleeping, I dreamed I held you in my arms....'" As Michael continued to sing, his baby sister relaxed, as if a healing rest had swept over her.

NICU nurses had gathered nearby. Some had tears in their eyes as they watched Michael and his sister.

"'You are my sunshine, my only sunshine ... please don't take my sunshine away.'"

Michael's sister amazed everyone. After Michael's visit, her heartbeat remained stable, her breathing was normal. She even began to gain weight. Within a short time she was strong enough to leave the NICU and go home with her family.

When I heard this story, I was struck by the power of love—the power of a little boy's love for his baby sister.

What I do know is that the kind of love that Michael had for his tiny sister—and that his mother had for both her children—is the key to a child's healthy development. Until we become parents, we would never believe how much we can love a child. And then it happens—our child is delivered into our arms, and we fall in love almost instantly!

Every child needs an adult who's crazy about her—who will put her welfare before career ambitions, the acquisition of things, a new relationship—someone crazy enough to love her unconditionally, who can form a strong relationship with her that lasts a lifetime.

As I pondered this powerful story, I was struck by the impact of the familiar song Michael sang to his baby sister in the NICU, how this infant's brain—long before birth—had been wired for music. I was struck by the resilience (what doctors call "plasticity") of the baby's brain—its ability to change and recover, and by the amazing capacity of the brain to respond to stimulation, particularly the special stimulation of her brother's song.

What a gift! What a wonder a baby is! What a miracle are the complex processes that produce talking, walking, seeing, and singing by the age of three or before. With the aid of high-tech brain scans that actually take pictures of a young child's brain at work, the secular world of medicine and neuroscience has begun to catch a glimpse of what God was describing long ago in Psalm 139:13–16 NLT that applies to each and every child:

> You made all the delicate, inner parts of my body
> and knit me together in my mother's womb.
> Thank you for making me so wonderfully complex!
> Your workmanship is marvelous—and how well I know it. . . .
> You saw me before I was born.
> Every day of my life was recorded in your book.
> Every moment was laid out before a single day had passed.

When our little ones come into the world, they are born with tremendous potential. Their brains contain billions of neurons eagerly waiting to complete and mature their connections with one another. This maturation process is influenced by all the experiences ahead—being hugged and cuddled and spoken to by Mom and Dad, seeing all the myriad colors, feeling textures, hearing all the sounds in the world around them. These neurons are not completely connected at birth. The more complex connections—the brain's "wiring" or "circuitry" that enables learning, thinking, and motor skills to function—are modified and completed after a child is born in response to specific environmental stimulation.

In this process of brain cell connection activity, children possess enormous potential to learn, grow, think, and create. God has prewired kids with the potential to develop in language so they could eventually speak several foreign languages, with the logical thinking potential to solve algebra or calculus problems, with the musical potential to someday play Vivaldi's "Pacabel Canon," and the spiritual capacity to know God and to love and pray for others, even at a young age. Because children are made in God's image and he is the Creator, he has placed the seed of creativity within them; he's prewired them with the curiosity that motivates them to crawl toward a bright toy, to discover things about space, to research the causes of world war.

Hearing about the incredible potential that your child has to learn, especially in the early years, may cause you to feel overwhelmed. So take a deep breath, and let's start at the beginning. We'll take a peek at what's happening in a child's brain at birth and during these critical "Learning Windows."

The Three M's

By the time your child is born, the first of three important M's has already been completed. The cells have "migrated," or traveled, to the areas of your baby's brain where they are designed to function—the language-designated cells to the language area, the logical thinking cells to their area, and other cells specially designed for the motor, musical, and other areas of the brain. This in itself is a miracle! You'd think all these cells would get confused running around in the young brain—but no! This is an orderly, although extremely energetic, process. And we're talking about a lot of cells—more than 100 billion—all raring to complete their learning pattern by being networked, wired, and influenced by the child's early experiences.

At birth the next M kicks into gear. This is "myelination"—a fancy word for the process of coating the fiber connections between nerve cells with insulating material called "myelin." These connecting fibers need to be protected because they carry a huge amount of electrical and chemical energy for the purpose of nerve cell communication and function.

The third M, "maturation," takes off when, as a result of stimulation, impulses pass from one neuron to another via a "synapse." Synaptic activity occurs when electrochemical energy arcs across a tiny space between nerve cell fibers, allowing these neurons to communicate and connect with one another, forming a "mapping" in the brain. With every "peekaboo" and "patty-cake" game, every bright color, every new word and song and motor skill performed, new connections are stimulated and reinforced by synaptic activity.

That's where you and I as parents come in—providing the stimulation and experiences that trigger those new circuits, or connections. As you'll see in the chapters ahead, I don't mean stimulation from expensive electronic toys, but the stimulation of loving, consistent care that forms emotional circuits—songs sung at bedtime that wire the musical part of the brain, conversations between mother and child throughout the day that cause new language circuits to grow. A child's experiences—whether he hears lots of music and interesting talk, receives eye contact and stimulation, has chances to ask questions, is encouraged to create projects and launch rockets or raise rabbits in the backyard to nurture curiosity—actually change the physiological development of his brain and shape the wiring of his brain cells.

You see, during the first three years when these M's are taking place, a child's brain grows to two-thirds of its adult size and is two and one-half times more active than the adult brain, creating electro-chemical synaptic activity at the speed of light. Full brain maturation is not actually complete until twelve to fourteen years of age; the possibilities for learning are amazing.

The Windows of Opportunity

In this time of explosive growth and networking of brain cells, there are prime times—windows of opportunity—when the brain is particularly ready and eager to gain specific new skills. We know so much more about these "windows" than we ever knew before. Educators used to think language began at one year when toddlers utter their first words, but now we know that months before that, they are learning language, expanding their vocabularies, and even learning grammatical patterns. We know that foreign languages are more easily learned in preschool or elementary school than in high school, and that if you want your child to speak a second language fluently without an accent, the child has to start learning that language early in life.

Preschoolers are at the top of the scale of curiosity, but their curiosity, unless stimulated, wanes by the time they're in junior high. While the majority of young children, when tested, measure "highly creative," only 2 percent of adults shine in the creative area. We know that few professional musicians began playing an instrument after the age of ten or twelve, and no world champion skater or golfer started learning their sport after age twelve. These facts indicate that there are windows of opportunity in a child's life.

How can you as a parent apply this new understanding of a child's potential? How can you make the most of these windows of opportunity? That's what this book is all about. You'll discover more about the marvelous capacity kids have in the early years to learn language, music, and logical thinking; to develop their creativity; to grow spiritually, physically, and emotionally; to develop their character. *Awareness* of these learning windows is a big part of making the most of the opportunities.

You'll get a "big picture" of your child's development as you read. But I've divided the information into manageable bites, with each chapter a different window of opportunity, a different "learning window." Each chapter is designed to show you how to stimulate a key area of your child's development. In the chapter on the Music Window, for example, you'll discover

- What's going on in babies and young children that's related to music.
- What we know about the musical abilities and sensitivity of kids.
- What you can do to enhance your child's development.

Maybe you've wanted to know different ways to help develop your child's music abilities, creativity, or math skills, but that's not your area of expertise. Be assured you don't have to be an expert in any of these areas to help your child grow in them!

Sometimes we actually hinder the very quality we want to nurture and encourage in our kids. Without realizing it, we do things that stifle, limit, or close a window of learning. Thus I've included in each chapter ways to avoid these "window closers," plus lists of helpful resources.

Instead of being overwhelmed, thinking you need to do all the activities in a given window of opportunity, take it one day at a time. The many suggested activities and resources provided for each window are not meant to all be done in one season or year. Pick a few ideas or an activity that sounds fun and enjoy it to the hilt with your child!

Be aware that there is some overlap in the chapters and the activities that build skills because there is overlap in the brain of the neurons used to process language, mathematics, music, and other windows. These skills aren't developed in isolation but in an integrated way. For example, a baby saying "Bye-bye" and waving a hand involves language and motor development. The baby's hand gesture reinforces the learning of the words. Music and language also are linked. Reciting vocabulary words to a tune strengthens memory, and a child not only learns the words faster but remembers them longer because of the music and the rhythm.

Although windows of potential learning are available for all children, the timetable is not the same for everyone. Every child has his own inner timetable when certain skills will develop or when talent will blossom. Every child is unique, wired differently than other kids. *Your child* is unique. He may excel in music while another child shines in language, logic, or physical abilities. That's why chapter 11 focuses on understanding these individual differences in personality and temperament, learning style, intelligence, and talents.

Be encouraged that it's never too late to foster healthy growth, to help your child learn. Although beginning to learn a foreign language or to play a musical instrument at the age of fifteen or thirty may take more effort and persistence than at age five—it can be done. Not only are researchers discovering that the best time for learning language, math, and music starts earlier than previously believed, they're also finding that these windows of learning may last longer than we thought.

For example, the auditory part of the brain that processes sound and language does so at a very rapid rate from birth through the first few years. But if opportunities are provided to enhance language skills, this high level of learning activity continues to age twelve and even into adolescence, when reasoning and critical thinking mature.

Although the potential for learning is greater in the first ten years of life, learning doesn't stop. As long as there are challenges and opportunities, the mind continues to learn throughout life, although at a slower rate as age increases. That's why it's never too late to provide the nurturing, conversation, music, and stimulating, interesting activities that help kids develop and learn and reach their potential.

Children are learning all the time! Their motivation to learn is divinely inspired, and brain development is happening constantly. You'll have a myriad of opportunities every day to provide experiences and interaction that will contribute to your child's learning and emerging gifts and talents. Many ideas in this book will help. So join me in the pages ahead as we explore the adventure of knowing and understanding your child's learning windows—starting with a petition for the help of the One who made them:

Lord, who formed the complexity
of the constellations and our universe
and the intricacy of our children's bodies and minds,
wonders that have kept scientists busy for centuries
attempting to unlock your mysteries,
thank you for the new discoveries that are helping us realize
the amazing potential in our children!
As I read, remind me that you are with me in this job of parenting,
every step of the way,
and give me your grace to make the most
of the windows of opportunity in my child's life!

LEARNING WINDOWS

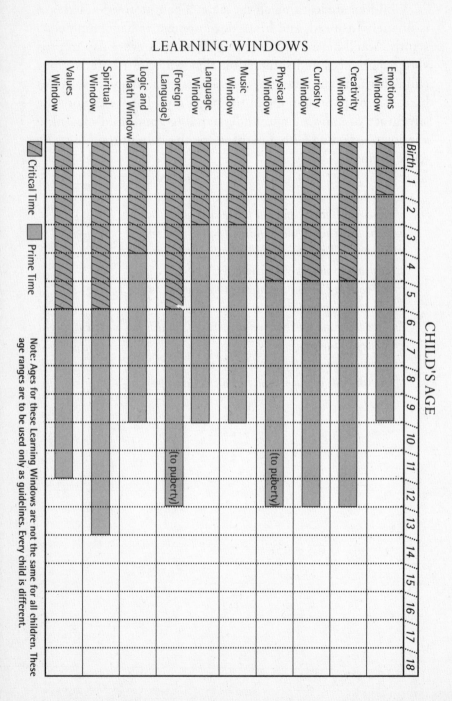

CHILD'S AGE

Learning Windows	Birth–1	2	3	4	5	6	7	8	9	10	11	12	13	14	15	16	17	18

Critical Time   Prime Time

Note: Ages for these Learning Windows are not the same for all children. These age ranges are to be used only as guidelines. Every child is different.

Two

the emotions window

The brain of a child who feels secure, loved, and happy can direct all its
attention toward learning and growth rather than focusing on worries and
fears. [1]

DR. JANE HEALY

"Da-da-da-ooh! Ooo—ooo!" seven-month-old Caitlin says.

"Da-da will be home tonight! Yes, da-da-da!" her mother, Tiffany, responds as she changes Caitlin's diaper. She playfully puts a clean, thin diaper across Caitlin's face and asks, "Where's Caitlin? Where can my baby be?"

Caitlin quickly pulls the cloth off and her face lights up. "Ee-ee-ooh!" she says melodically, waving her arms up and down.

"Peekaboo, Caitlin! I see you!" Tiffany says, smiling at her baby as she finishes dressing her and picks her up into a big hug.

All the interaction between mother and baby—the loving vocalization, the play and eye contact, a mother responding to and mimicking her baby's babbling, the gentle physical touching—plays an important role in emotional nurturing and growth. In just those brief moments of interaction, neurons in Caitlin's brain were connected with other neurons, and existing connections between cells were strengthened, adding to the vital circuitry of emotional wiring.

What We Know About the Emotions Window

Just as babies' brains are wired for language, music, and logic, they are also wired for emotions and feelings. In fact, some of the first and most important circuits the brain develops are those governing feelings—and this emotional wiring impacts how children develop mentally, socially, and morally. A child's emotional development impacts how that child relates to other people, how well they can control their own emotions, how well they pay attention in the classroom, and a host of other skills. Here's a sampling of what we know about the Emotions Window:

Time Span

The prime time for emotional wiring is birth to age ten. During that time the brain sets up the circuitry needed to experience and handle emotions that range from joy and sadness to envy, empathy, and anxiety.

Layers of Emotions

Emotions develop in layers, each more complex than the last.[2] In the first weeks and months, babies experience moments of sheer contentment when their needs are met, and moments of frustration and distress when they're not. Their emotions become increasingly complex as they grow: fear and anger, envy and empathy, rivalry and anxiety. By their first birthday, children are experiencing and expressing many emotions. The different feelings are wired at different times. For example, empathy develops early, between the ages of two to three, whereas the emotion of guilt develops later, around the age of four.

Coping Skills

All kids experience some fearfulness, whether it's fear of dogs, or nightmares, or thunderstorms, or anxiety about separation from Mom and Dad. One of the challenges of parenting is to help our children learn how to deal with whatever emotion they are experiencing without being overwhelmed, crippled, or controlled.

Emotional Signals

Babies use cries, screams, and facial expressions to convey feelings, but by about the age of two, they begin adding words and other cues to express anger, frustration, jealousy, and joy.

An Emotional Leap

By approximately eight months, the frontal cortex (the part of the brain associated with the ability to regulate and express emotions, to think and plan) shows a large increase in activity. Interestingly, at the time this is happening, babies are also strengthening their attachment to their primary caregiver. This is a time to respond very sensitively to their emotional signals.[3]

Mood Swings

In the first year of life, children develop a fundamental attitude toward life that is optimistic or pessimistic, hopeful or despairing, happy or unhappy.

Emotional Stimulation

Emotional wiring or development is fostered by loving, nurturing care from a consistent person (usually the mother and/or father) that builds a secure bond or attachment. Emotional stimulation such as breast-feeding and cuddling, singing songs and lullabies, responding to a baby with smiles and hugs, and engaging in play all help to build that secure bond.

Attunement

Perhaps the strongest emotional stimulation needed for good brain development is what researchers call "attunement," when the parent or other adult plays back the child's inner feelings and responds appropriately. Attunement means being "tuned in" to your child's cues and clues, noticing her moods, understanding what's going on, and responding in a way that fosters emotional growth. It's knowing when a baby needs comfort and when she needs stimulation, knowing when she needs help calming down or encouragement to adapt to a new situation.

For example, if a baby's joy at the sight and sound of a new toy is met with your smile and verbal affirmation of shared delight, circuits for the feeling of joy or happiness are reinforced. If your baby's colic distress is met by your comforting, rocking, and soothing her, she eventually learns to calm herself down and the emotions that build trust are reinforced. But if a baby's expressions of joy or pain are not responded to or are neglected by parents, emotional and mental growth can be stifled and even damaged. Daniel Goleman, author of *Emotional Intelligence* and a writer for the *New York Times* who covers the behavioral and brain sciences, says that all the emotional exchanges between parent and child during a child's growing-up years form the core of the child's emotional outlook and capabilities.[4]

A Baby's Stress

Babies and young children need more help handling certain emotions than they do others. A new research study at the University of Wisconsin at Madison showed that babies have a harder time calming down after being frightened than after being angry, and need more cuddling and reassurance to deal with their fear. The researchers, who videotaped twelve- and eighteen-month-old babies during situations that made them angry or afraid, made some interesting observations. When angry, the babies were able to calm down by just looking at their mother or being distracted by a toy or something in the room. But when the babies were frightened by a spider moving toward them, they couldn't be consoled by

TIP: In stressful situations, such as a family move to another town or hospitalization of a grandparent, give your baby or young child lots of attention and tender loving care. This increases your child's sense of security and helps to protect your child from excess stress, even in very trying times.

either Mom's presence or by being distracted. One sign that a baby has reached her limit and is faced with more stress than she has the ability to handle is when she's unable to calm down.

Reaction to Parents' Emotions

Babies and young children are very sensitive to parents' emotions, their verbal and nonverbal emotional cues, and they react to them. Even our littlest children pay attention to parents' facial expressions and tone of voice. For example, the mother of a nine-month-old is very anxious around strangers. Sensing the mother's tension, the baby begins to cry whenever the mother is in a situation where she is close to strangers. When you are overstressed or irritable, your child perceives the tension in your voice and picks up signals from how you hold her. Babies are also impacted by parental depression. Infants of chronically depressed mothers tend to be more withdrawn and less active than other babies. When the mother's depression is treated, the babies' brain activity returns to normal.[5]

Individual Differences

Babies and young children show wide individual differences in emotionality. An easy, or placid, infant (what we often call "a good baby") may seem cheerful most of the time. New situations don't seem to ruffle her happy mood and she adapts easily. Another baby is fussier, needing more comfort and attention—a "high-maintenance" baby. Some kids are very intense and expressive with their emotions and others are more mild-mannered. In chapter 11 we'll look more at the temperament, the learning style, and the individual differences in children and how these affect your interaction with your children.

Babies who are "emotionally competent" have gotten a big dose of approval and encouragement from the adults in their lives; they expect to succeed in life's little challenges, says Goleman in his book *Emotional Intelligence.*[6] This confident, optimistic outlook is a significant sign of emotional health. Kids who lack encouragement and approval in the early years, on the other hand, tend to expect failure in the challenges they face.

Warm, responsive care isn't a "want" for babies and young children, it's a "need" that's critical for healthy development.[7] When kids get consistent loving care in their early years, they are able to learn and develop to their potential, they tend to develop healthy social skills, and they're more resilient and able to handle stress and trauma in their lives. In other words, emotional stability is significantly affected by how the brain is wired emotionally during the first few years. From a baby's earliest days to the teen years, loving care provides the kind of emotional stimulation the brain needs to grow.

What You Can Do: Emotional Basics

If emotional development is the cornerstone of children's learning and growth, and the years from birth to age ten are a prime time for emotional nurturing, how can we provide the basics children need to develop in this window of opportunity?

Bonding

The first step is developing a healthy bond, or attachment, with our child. Research in the 1970s by British psychiatrist Dr. John Bowlby and many studies since then show the importance of an infant's attachment to the mother or primary caregiver, what happens when a child loses or is separated from her mother or fails to develop a secure bond, and how early attachment affects a child's later relationships. Now with brain-imaging technologies, neuroscientists can actually gauge attachment and detect the effects of caregivers' responsive, warm care or its absence on the brain's biochemistry and architecture.[8]

Although emotional development is taking place during the childhood years up to age ten, the first two years of life hold the key for attachment. Loving, sensitive, responsive care from the mother, the father, or a consistent caregiver in the first year of life is at the core of a secure attachment, and by the second birthday, researchers can identify whether kids are securely attached or not.

An interesting new study at the State University of New York at Geneseo reinforced the notion that establishing a close bond with your baby lays the foundation for his cognitive development. The researchers observed preschoolers who were securely attached to their mothers and those who were insecurely attached. Two years later they found the ability to comprehend and remember details from stories they were read was significantly higher in the attached children. The researchers concluded that the children's early relationships shaped how they processed information. When babies develop a secure bond, they have a lasting visual image of their parents and the world as being responsive to their needs. Without this basic attachment, kids expect their needs won't be met.[9]

The importance of a loving attachment comes into perspective when we look at young people who lack that bond. As experts have tried to figure out why more delinquents and violent children are coming from average homes with hardworking, noncriminal parents, there's one common factor they're finding: in their early, formative years, their caregivers were persistently unresponsive or emotionally unavailable.[10] These kids didn't develop a bond with either parent or with any other adult.[11] In the hectic, fast-moving pace of life, no one focused on them and their needs. No one took time to talk to them and listen to them, helping them discover who they are and how to deal constructively with their emotions. These children grew up unattached emotionally and didn't learn how to give or receive love in healthy, constructive ways. They often developed learning difficulties and aggression problems at school and in the neighborhood.

The attachment between parent and child in the early years is so important that Thomas Lickona, a developmental psychologist, calls it the "indispensable basis for later moral development."[12] Without a loving, trusting connection with parents, kids don't develop a sense of right and wrong. They lack a conscience and so can commit cruel acts without regret or any feeling for the victim.

We find emotional growth—or the lack of it—dramatically impacts a child's ability to learn. A report from the National Center for Clinical Infant Programs discovered seven key ingredients of a child's readiness to learn and *all* of them relate to emotional growth: confidence, curiosity, intentionality, self-control, relating to others, capacity to communicate, and capacity to cooperate.[13]

We can see that forming a secure attachment is vital. All the hugging and cuddling, nursing and nurturing it takes to meet your baby's needs in the cradle help him to investigate the world, communicate, play, read, and interact with siblings and friends as he grows.

Adoption presents a special concern in the realm of attachment. Even though the decision to adopt is a very loving one, the child may suffer from feelings of abandonment. How can this be minimized and a strong bond with the adoptive family be established?

Any type of object that tangibly represents the underpinnings of love that nurtured the decision to give the child up for adoption can greatly benefit a young child. A small gift from the birthparents, such as a teddy bear or a book, provides the adopted child with a transitional object to represent their acceptance by the birthparents even though they gave up the child for adoption. A letter from the birthparents to share with the child when that child is ready to receive the information would be excellent.

The adoptive family can provide special events to mark the child's acceptance into his new family. For example, I have a friend who emphasizes the day her children were adopted by celebrating their adoption days. The celebration is complete with an adoption-day cake, balloons, streamers, and one special present. The gift is usually an item that the child has longed for over a period of time. Before the child opens his present, my friend and her husband will remind their child that no matter how happy he is to receive his special gift, they were even more excited to have him become their very own son! The door of discussion is formally opened and they will ask if he has any questions about his birthfamily. If the time is not appropriate to answer all the questions, the child is encouraged to ask the same question the next year.

The wise parent will talk openly about adoption and spontaneously discuss whatever issues and questions may arise through daily life. Many wonderful books are available to explain the concept of adoption to children of all ages. (See the list of resources at the end of the chapter.)

Time Together

The next emotional parenting "basic," which overlaps with bonding and attachment, is time together. You've perhaps heard the saying that to kids, love is spelled T-I-M-E, but it bears repeating. In the years following the close and active nurturing of infants, kids continue to need their parents' attention.

"Parents' most important gift to their child is not a good education, elaborate educational toys, or summer camp, but time—regular, substantial chunks of it spent together doing things that are naturally appealing to the child," says Dr. Stanley Greenspan in *The Growth of the Mind*.[14]

How can a busy parent give the gift of time to her child? As a young mother with three children to care for, part-time teaching, and a husband who needed my help in his business from time to time, plus laundry and cooking and all the responsibilities that running a household entail, I wondered that! One of the most helpful concepts I discovered was how to fill up my children's emotional tanks.

Kids have a wide-open place in their hearts (think "gas tank that needs to be filled"), I learned from Dr. Ross Campbell's book *How to Really Love Your Teenager*.[15] This "tank" isn't filled by McDonald's Happy Meals, ice-cream treats, or even new toys or expensive gadgets, because it's an *emotional* tank. Thus the fuel my children needed to fill their empty tanks was "focused attention," which Campbell calls "full, undivided attention in such a way that he feels truly loved, that he knows he is so valuable in his own right that he warrants your watchfulness, appreciation, and uncompromising regard."[16]

This refilling might happen during a brief time of sitting on the floor and playing with my then preschooler Alison, or playing catch with Chris while chatting about his school day, or sitting on the side of Justin's bed after lights-out to listen, pray, and give him a back rub. When they were younger, it happened when I nursed and rocked them to sleep or played "peekaboo" as Tiffany did with her baby, but it changed as they grew.

No, this "focused attention" didn't happen every day, and it didn't mean the kids had my undivided attention all day, but a funny thing happened after I began putting into regular practice this refueling of my kids' emotional tanks: I discovered they were whining less, bugging each other less, and sometimes before I was through with our tender time of reading together or doing a puzzle or board game, they popped up and got busy with their own projects— apparently refilled and ready to go!

What you and your child enjoy doing may be hiking or camping, collecting rocks, reading together, playing tennis or Frisbee, flying a kite, or working on a model plane. It all depends on you and your youngster's individual interests. And it's different at age five than it is at fifteen; needs change.

Parents can do a myriad of simple things with toddlers and preschoolers, things that are cheap and available right at home— because the great thing about little ones is they enjoy doing *almost anything* with Mom or Dad and it doesn't have to cost money. Baking cookies, floor play, walking the dog, folding laundry together, cuddling in bed reading a story, or going to the park are all enjoyable.

These activities can provide opportunities to talk, listen, and just be together. If the time together involves play, all the better because play is an important part of the bonding process in any relationship, especially with kids. Play is also how children learn. When you ask, "Where's baby?" and play "Peekaboo, I see you," your child learns that although he can't see you, you are there— you disappear for a few seconds, then magically return. Shared activities, no matter how ordinary or the age of your child, build bridges of communication, connection, and love between parent and child.

Physical Touch

We've already said that touch is important to the development of babies and children. Physical touch not only has emotional benefits but it also stimulates the central nervous system, boosts the immune system, and reduces stress. The power of touch has been shown vividly with premature babies. The preemies who have physical contact with parents and extra doses of cuddling and massage from nurses gain weight faster, digest food better, and develop better motor skills.[17]

Physical affection meets some of a child's emotional needs not only in infancy but throughout a child's growing-up years. Kids often need physical affection the most when they are the *least lovable*—when they're irritable and under stress, have had a hard day at school, or been put down by a friend. Hugs, pats, and cuddles fill up kids' emotional tanks so they have the energy they need to tackle the challenges of growing up.

The Magic of Encouragement

An important part of emotional nurturing centers on providing an atmosphere of encouragement in the family. The child who is encouraged develops confidence and courage to face difficulties.

Many studies show that children who are encouraged at home are more motivated at school, that those who have the inner strength to keep trying despite obstacles have parents who are like quiet cheerleaders—they have positive expectations but aren't demanding. If their child fails in some undertaking, these parents aren't negative or critical. They talk about the failure, and the child is encouraged to learn from the experience and to try again. Positive words, smiles, listening, talking, and physical affection are frequent. The parents share in their child's excitement and interests. And the most important secret of all—they cheer and appreciate all of their child's efforts, not just his abilities and successes. This kind of encouragement nurtures emotional growth.

Boundaries Build Emotional Security

Part of emotional parenting is setting limits and boundaries for your child so that she feels protected and secure. How important are boundaries? Dr. Henry Cloud and Dr. John Townsend, in their book *Boundaries*, say, "Parenting with love and limits, with warmth and consequences, produces confident children who have a sense of control over their lives."[18] So great was the need of parents to know more about how to set boundaries in their families that Cloud and Townsend wrote *Boundaries with Kids*. I highly recommend it.

Boundaries, healthy discipline, and limit-setting aren't contrary to affection and secure attachment—in fact, one is essential for the other. Someone said that trying to raise kids without boundaries and limits is like putting a man on top of a very tall building without railings in the darkest night and saying, "Just walk around, do whatever you want, and have a blast!" It breeds insecurity and anxiety to live with no limits. That's why permissive parenting often produces kids who aren't sure of themselves or don't know how to control themselves.

Children do need specific guidelines and rules for acceptable behavior, but keep the rules realistic (those you can and will enforce), majoring on the "majors" instead of the "minors" so that you're not saying "no" constantly. Use natural and logical consequences when rules are broken, asserting your parental authority firmly, lovingly, and quietly.

Being Emotionally Available

Work on your own issues so you will be emotionally available to your child. I could suggest you hug your child eight times a day (the recommended hug quota per day for just adequate mental health), but if you're frozen inside because of your own unresolved issues, it may be difficult for you and your child to connect emotionally. If parents have constant emotions like anger, bitterness, or anxiety weighing them down, they tend to distance themselves from present events and people—even their own children—and not be emotionally available for them. It's like trying to look through fogged-up windows in a car and having a hard time seeing out.

Forgiving those who have hurt you and resolving conflicts in relationships can do much to clear the window of your heart. Releasing daily worries, disappointments, and fears can also be helpful—writing down the problems you're worried about (talking with someone if possible), praying about them, and then letting go of them. I've sometimes found I had to release a problem many times after it kept creeping back into my thoughts. But when I had really let it go and wasn't mulling over it anymore, not only was there renewed energy for my kids but often that's when a creative solution occurred to me.

Being emotionally available also means being at peace with yourself and with your own emotional makeup (your strengths and weaknesses). "There's a common pattern among caring parents," says Dr. Ken Wilgus, a psychologist specializing in adolescent and family counseling. "When you see the emotional patterns you dislike in yourself—patterns you've tried to control or deny—and then recognize them in your child, you'll tend to overreact instead of helping him deal with his emotions or behavior constructively."

For example, when Ken's son Alex was born, he was prepared for him to be strong-willed and assertive but felt with his counseling experience, he could deal with that—no problem. Instead Alex was soft-tempered and sensitive—characteristics Ken possesses and hates in himself. Being ashamed of his own sensitivity, Ken tended to overreact to Alex's sometimes whiny or tearful softheartedness. He found, as he came to peace with his own emotional makeup and particularly this quality of softheartedness, that he accepted the way God had made Alex and could better help him deal with his sensitive nature.

Coaching Your Child on Emotions

When we show our kids how to handle stress, blue moods, anger, and frustration, we're instilling emotional habits that will be valuable throughout their lives. Here are some ways to coach in a healthy way:

- Before reacting, step back and listen to get a good feel for where your child is. Instead of projecting your emotions on him or telling him how he feels, pay attention to how he's reacting.
- Take some time away with the child, perhaps even physically away from the home or situation, and let conversation develop (instead of trying to have an instant "30 Second Managing the Situation" kind of talk). In the car (where many kids, especially preteens, are more responsive), or on a walk, or shooting baskets, talk can open up. Use some "feeling" words to reflect back what you're hearing: "It sounds like you're feeling frustrated . . ." or "You're really angry about that . . ."
- Some situations don't have a "fix-it" solution, but if problem-solving is needed, prompt your child to suggest a few possible ideas. Then encourage his participation in evaluating the solutions.

Facing What Is Out of Our Control

Let me balance all that's been said in this chapter by passing on what Ken Wilgus shared with me as we talked about this topic at his family's Texas farm: When it comes to emotional parenting, we can avoid gross errors, but there are certain things out of our control.

One factor is the individual differences in children and their own process of attachment. If you have four children, you may care for them in very similar ways, but their ability to "attach," or bond, may vary according to their personality makeup and their experience. Ken finds in his practice that the ability to attach is related in some ways to kids' ability to "attend." You can spend the same amount of "TLC," or focused time, with two children. One is more tuned in and cuddly—giving and receiving eye contact, listening and talking with you—and thus soaks up the nurturing. The other, with a shorter attention span, may not experience the security and closeness because he's flitting about or just not "attending" to your verbal and nonverbal nurturing.

Another factor has to do with the circumstances of your life. When our middle child, Chris, was a year old, his big brother, Justin, began having severe asthma attacks and was hospitalized for up to a week each time. When I had to be at the hospital with Justin, Chris went to his grandmother's house an hour away or was cared for at home by his dad. I couldn't control or change those circumstances, but they did impact both sons. Chris grew more independent and, although we had a good bond, he also developed a close relationship with his grandmother, who often cared for him when his brother was hospitalized. Justin had a chronic illness to deal with—something we'd never planned. In the midst of sometimes difficult circumstances, I found over and over that God's grace covers the gaps in our children's lives as well as in our own.

Prayer and Your Child's Development

In wrapping up this chapter, here's a helpful way to pray specifically for the developmental stages as your children pass through them:

Infancy through toddlerhood: You can pray that your infant will develop trust and a strong sense of security as he bonds with you and other significant family members. As you're rocking him, feeding him, and maybe, most of all, when you're trying to comfort him in the middle of the night, these prayers can remind you of how precious this time together is.

Toddlerhood: You can pray that your children will develop a healthy sense of independence. In these years children begin to see themselves as more distinct from others. They are developing a self-concept. Recognizing and appreciating this stage of autonomy may help you react with patience as your two-year-old's favorite word becomes "No!"

Early childhood: In these years you might specifically pray for your children to develop a healthy curiosity, to learn to play well with others, to explore and create without fear of failure.

School age: From ages seven to ten, the "industry" stage, ask God to help your children discover their God-given gifts and talents, to develop a sense of satisfaction and joy in using their skills so that they believe "I can do this. I have something to contribute." This is also a critical time for the development of their conscience.[19]

Pray for yourself, too: Pray that you will see your child with the Father's eyes, accept her fully, and respond to her with God's love, that you will see into the windows of your child's heart and discover her needs and, with the Lord's wisdom and strength, fill them.

Emotions Window Closers to Avoid

Look at your child with the Father's eyes. Don't limit how you see your child by assigning a positive or negative label. Labels can blind parents to areas of excellence or concern that need to be addressed. Besides, children tend to live up (or down) to the labels assigned to them.

Put margins of time into your day for unexpected emergencies. Nothing destroys relationships quicker than unrealistic expectations. When you are stressed and rushing out the door, late for an appointment, you are in danger of being sent over the emotional edge and reacting in a hurtful way to your child. How would you react if, in that hurry to leave, your five-year-old spilled a glass of milk all over herself?

In stressful moments, count to ten, take deep breaths, and pray for help. Take a time-out before you act out in anger.

When there is family stress or tragedy, provide help for kids to work through their feelings. On a television interview, a distressed mother told me about her sixth grader who had once been a good student but, starting around the third grade, began having major problems at school and was failing everything.

"What happened to your child in third grade—were there any special stresses on the family?" I asked. I soon discovered the child's sibling had died that year, and the adults had been so busy with their own pain they were not available to help their daughter through her grief. When there's a death, divorce, or major calamity or stress in a family, the children need a guide to walk them out of the jungle of feelings, someone with the knowledge and personal strength to listen and provide support. Often parents want to encourage kids to hurry and "snap out of it," and their feelings end up stuffed down inside, with resulting long-term effects.

Avoid overinvolvement. When parents are so involved emotionally with their child that they express everything for the child, the child lacks any motivation to express feelings. For example, the kids are opening Christmas packages and the ten-year-old opens a gift from his uncle, who is present. Mom says, "Oh, isn't that great—a NASA space set! How wonderful! Thanks, Uncle John! Won't this be fun? We love this!" The son has no need to express his feelings or appreciation for the gift— Mom already has!

Avoid hanging on. I think letting go is one of the hardest parts of parenting, at least for mothers. But when the time comes to give "wings" to this child you've worked so hard to give "roots," let him know you're going to be OK emotionally. When one mom told her teenager, "You're my only reason for continuing on," the daughter, instead of looking forward to leaving for college in two years, began to dread it. Although it's hard for parents (especially for us moms) when our children separate from us in order to learn to stand on their own two feet, that's what we're preparing them for, and it's the natural, divinely inspired process!

As we entrust our kids to the One who fearfully and wonderfully made them, doing our part as parents while trusting him not only with the outcome of their emotional lives but also with their mental, physical, and spiritual development, we'll find peace in the challenging job of parenting!

Resources to Encourage Conversation

Children's books can help a child grow in expressing feelings with parents. They can encourage conversation about events or situations that often trigger strong emotions like losing a grandparent, being hospitalized, moving to a new town, having a new baby in the family, adoption, or dealing with everyday anger, fear, or silliness.

Tell Me Again About the Night I Was Born by Jamie Lee Curtis (New York: Joanna Cotler Books, 1996).

Today I Feel Silly and Other Moods That Make My Day by Jamie Lee Curtis (New York: Joanna Cotler Books, 1998).

The Saddest Time by Norma Simon (Morton Grove, Ill.: Albert Whitman & Co., 1986).

The New Baby at Your House by Joanne Cole (New York: Mulberry Books, 1985).

Going to the Hospital by Fred Rogers (New York: The Putnam & Grosset Group, 1988).

How I Was Adopted by Joanne Cole (New York: Morrow Junior Books, 1995).

Why Was I Adopted? by Carole Livingston (Secaucus, N.J.: Carol Publishing Group, 1996).

Fear Not! A Story of Hope by Monica Hall (Nashville: Tommy Nelson, 1998).

Moving Gives Me a Stomach Ache by Heather McKend (Windsor: Black Moss Press, 1988).

I Was So Mad! by Norma Simon (Morton Grove, Ill.: Albert Whitman & Co., 1974).

My Many Colored Days by Dr. Seuss (New York: Alfred A. Knopf, 1996).

I Love to Cuddle by Carl Norac (New York: Doubleday, 1998).

I Love You the Purplest by Barbara M. Joosee (San Francisco: Chronicle Books, 1996).

Lord, remind my heart in this awesome responsibility of parenting
that I have nothing to fear, for you are my shield.
Cause me to grow so much in knowing you
and experiencing your Father's love
that I can love my child unconditionally.
Give me the energy and wisdom I need
to provide boundaries and limits and meet my child's emotional needs,
with a daily dependence on you
as my main counselor, comforter, and friend.

Three

the creativity window

Imagination is more important than knowledge.

ALBERT EINSTEIN

Roman and Ramsey Brown, two imaginative brothers who live in Texas, were brainstorming during family devotions one night about ways to be kind to people when the topic got narrowed down to showing kindness and love to their *parents*. Mom and Dad encouraged the boys to think up different, creative ideas instead of just run-of-the-mill ones. Roman and Ramsey got going with pen and paper, adding to the list during the summer. Their project became a book recently published by Garborg's entitled *101 Ways Kids Can Spoil Their Parents.*[1]

The book includes such innovative suggestions as: "Help take care of them when they're sick (You might tell them you're willing to stay home from school to help)." "Make a cake on your Mom's and Dad's birthday, but don't mention their age (They get real sensitive about this)." Guess what? *101 Ways* is selling like hotcakes, and two sequels are on the way. The royalties are being socked away in trust funds for the boys' college education. You never know where problem-solving and creative brainstorming will take you and your child.

Since our children are made by an incredibly creative God, each one is unique and creative, with a one-of-a-kind brain, special talents and gifts, and different ways of looking at life. Although kids come into the world extremely creative—as witnessed by the many colors they can fingerpaint walls if unsupervised—something happens to derail this potential. Did you know that when kindergarten children's imaginative potential was evaluated, *90 percent* measured *"highly creative"?*

You've probably observed this creativity if you spend much time with kids. While corporate trainers spend millions to get CEOs to think creatively (using what they call "divergent thinking"), little kids engage in it naturally. This out-of-the-box kind of thinking was evident during a lesson on magnets. The first-grade teacher did an experiment demonstrating magnetism, gave explanations of the principles of magnetism, and had students complete a worksheet on magnets. Then she tested them. She asked the class: "My name starts with M, has six letters, and I pick up things. What am I?"

Half the students answered, "Mother!"

Unfortunately, most of those creative-thinking first graders aren't going to stay that way very long. Surveys show that the number of kids measuring "highly creative" drops to 20 percent by age seven or eight, and among adults only 2 percent measure highly creative. What this tells me is there is a window of opportunity in the early years—let's call it the "Creativity Window," when children are naturally thinking and doing imaginative things. During the Creativity Window, kids' minds are ripe for creative development.

To make the most of this window of opportunity, let's look first at what creativity is, what we know about creativity in kids and adults, and what we can do to encourage and nurture its growth in our children.

The Gift of Creativity

Creativity isn't just being artistic with drawing or writing flowery poetry. It's also a building block for problem-solving and for critical and divergent thinking. Creativity is a "synthesizing" ability—the ability to combine different experiences or ideas and see them in a new way. It's the ability to look at an old problem and come up with an entirely new solution, much like a California boy named Chris Haas did when he came up with the idea for "Hands On Basketball."

As a nine-year-old, Chris saw that kids at school had trouble knowing how to shoot the ball effectively or even where to put their hands. So he stuck his hands in poster paint and put them on a basketball, right where they needed to be—which helped kids sink shots. The "Hands On" balls he created were so popular Chris added a "Hands On Football" and both are now trademarked and marketed nationally.[2]

Creative thinking happens in every field of work or endeavor. There's creative writing, creative advertising, engineering feats, and inventions that come purely out of imaginative and creative thought, and computer programs birthed in someone's mind. It takes creative thinking to figure out a cure for disease and solve problems in the business world as well as to create in the arts, in music, dance, the visual arts, and theater. Creativity knows no age barriers. A young seven-year-old cook named Justin has been exercising his creativity in the kitchen since he was a toddler and has published cookbooks and made numerous television appearances.

Creativity is a fascinating mix of components or abilities such as originality, flexibility, the ability for imaginative or visual thinking, curiosity, divergent thinking, and the ability to generate a number of different ideas about a subject.

How does this imaginative quality develop?

What We Know: Creativity Unfolding

Every Child Is Creative

In traditional schooling's standardized testing, only 5 percent of students are selected as "gifted, creative, and talented." So if your child doesn't fall in that elite group, you may not have realized his potential. Actually, creativity is an inborn quality that *all* people possess to some degree because we are made in the image of a creative God—and that creativity is generally expressed best in our individual areas of talent and intelligence. What differs is whether that creativity is nurtured.

"The kernel of creativity is there in the infant: the desire and drive to explore, to find out about things, to try things out, to experiment with different ways of handling things and looking at things," says psychologist Teresa Amabile. "As they grow older, children begin to create entire universes of reality in their play."[3]

Creativity in Childhood Shapes Creativity in Adulthood

The experience kids have of creativity in their growing-up years shapes much of what they do in adulthood, from work to family life.[4] If their creativity is nurtured and given opportunities to grow, it will enhance and enrich whatever interests, pursuits, or career they engage in later in life. People tend to exhibit creativity in the areas in which they have strengths, intelligence, and talent. If music is their bent, that's where creativity would show itself; if writing or science is their forte, that's where they would express their creativity and originality.

Kids Don't Have to Be Taught to Be Creative; They Already Are

Encouraging creativity isn't like teaching your child the ABCs. Since kids' whole approach to learning and life is creative exploration, it's more a matter of providing resources, time, and encouragement to continue doing what they do naturally.

Brain scientists report that the brain wave pattern of children is abundant in "theta waves," the same waves that characterize adults' dreamlike states—that magical time between sleeping and waking when some of our best "Aha!" moments of creativity or inventiveness occur.

"With puberty, the child's brain changes to resemble an adult's. The theta brain waves and the wildly creative flair of the child begin to fade," says Daniel Goleman in *The Creative Spirit*.[5]

Children Show Intense Absorption in Activities

Children often exhibit an intense absorption in their activities while playing something or doing something that is personally fascinating to them. This "flow," or absorption, which is part of the essence of creativity, is often derailed by us adults when we say, "C'mon! We've got to go. Stop doing that. I've got to get to an appointment."

When our son Chris was a preschooler, he could "get lost" for big blocks of time as he made an Indian costume, created a multi-room house out of boxes, or built an intricate-looking space ship out of LEGOs. It took all the patience I could muster to allow him to complete his creation before we moved on to the next thing that needed to be done.

While we often overgeneralize and label young children as having short attention spans, the truth is that, just as Chris spent long periods of time engrossed in making his latest creation, kids can have amazingly long attention for an activity *if it's something they initiate and are interested in*. In fact, this concentration is much like the "flow" state at the height of the creative process when a person is so absorbed in poetry-writing, painting, or his baseball swing that he isn't aware of anything else.

> **TIP:** Instead of interrupting your child when she's lost in a creative pursuit, try to exercise some patience, allowing her to finish what she's doing, and you'll be fostering her creative spirit.

Forcing Creativity Can Kill It

You can't demand, pressure, or push kids to perform in the arena of creativity. Dr. Jane Healy suggests that "presenting advance practices or theory in the hopes of accelerating development is useless. Telling a child what to do to produce a pretty product will make him dependent on your direction and unsure of his own aesthetic choices."[6]

Creative Thinking Involves Making Connections

Your child's creative thinking involves making "connections" between movement, the senses, and ideas. In preschool children, these connections, or "links," are best made by using their bodies

and a hands-on approach in the creative process (like fingerpaint-
ing or engaging in pretend play), which helps coordinate both right
and left hemisphere thinking.[7]

Creativity Doesn't Have to Diminish with Age

Creativity is much like the relationship of exercise to your metabolism, muscle strength, and fitness. If you use it, you won't lose it. Creativity doesn't have to diminish or slow down as your child gets older.
If your child continues having opportunities to exercise her creativity,
her creativity can be expressed for a lifetime. Even if your child hasn't
had many opportunities to engage in the creative process, you can take
heart. It's never too late to begin, and there are lots of ideas to try and
helpful resources listed in this chapter and throughout the book.

Artistic Skills Are Developmental

Toddlers begin with scribbling and swirling colors and lines; they
aren't concerned about realism. By scribbling, they learn to manipulate and play with colors and develop their fine motor skills. By age
three, kids' artwork is more intentional; they repeat patterns and
shapes, and their color selection gets even more vivid. They also begin
to describe their drawings verbally and draw figures that represent and
actually look like real objects, such as animals and flowers. At ages four
and five, fine motor skills are sharper and kids put more detail into
their pictures. They use their art to tell a story or express a feeling.

Playful Ideas Build Creativity and Imagination

That's why *play* is so important to the nurturing of children's
natural creativity. Let's look at ways to encourage this wonderful
God-given quality, starting with playing with your child.

What You Can Do: Nurturing Creativity

Play with Your Children

That may be a foreign word for some of us work-oriented, productive grown-ups, but having recently become a grandmother, I've

rediscovered the fun of "floor play." That's when I leave my computer to sit on a colorful quilt with our grandbaby Caitlin and do all sorts of fun things: play musical toys, have a sing-along, blow bubbles, or throw Beanie Baby rabbits in the air, all to get Caitlin to laugh in that contagious way I love to hear and to just watch her play with the toys surrounding her. Curiously, after some quilt time with Caitlin, I often find when I return to my writing that my mind is fresher and new ideas come easier! In a childlike spirit, try some floor time playing with your child. If she's graduated from the quilt and baby days, follow her lead and have a pretend tea party or imagine you're astronauts going into outer space.

Keep the Raw Materials for Creativity Handy

Set aside a project room or even a table or a corner of a room or garage for creative projects. Bright-colored bins work well for holding unusual and ordinary raw materials of creativity (with a vinyl tablecloth and maybe a drop cloth on the floor for spills). For making collages, collect scraps of fabric, feathers, yarn, gift wrap, string and buttons, seeds and macaroni. Keep a supply of egg cartons and plastic foam trays, clay, colored paper, markers, cardboard tubes, glitter, and pipe cleaners. Odds and ends of junk to invent things (for some kids, that could even include old toasters and small engines to take apart), dress-up clothes, and garage sale "finds" are all great additions to the creativity center.

Provide the Gift of Time

One of the biggest hindrances to children's developing creativity is a lack of time. In the hurry-up world we live in, we rush kids from one place to another and another—all good activities but sometimes too many of them in the same week—with little or no time left for them to dream or read or pursue their own interests.

It takes time and patience to make things, play, draw a picture, create a new recipe, or get absorbed in inventing something with kids. Often when our child gets really "into" a project, we whisk him off to another scheduled event, which brings frustration and stifles creativity.

So let me encourage you to go against the hectic, fast-forward grain of our society and give your child the *gift of time* (one of the best contributions you can make to his developing imagination and creativity)—time to watch the sunset, time to study a bunch of clouds and talk about what the clouds look like, time to sit by a glowing fireplace and read about an island paradise on the other side of the world, time to fly a kite, make mud pies, silly sculptures, and card table tents.

Talk with Your Children

Anytime you talk with your children instead of watching television, the conversation is sharpening their creativity. That's because creative thinking includes skills like problem-solving, predicting outcomes, drawing conclusions, and creating analogies. Debates— where you discuss the pros and cons of whether Disney World or a mountain backpacking trip would be a better family getaway—are a great way to practice these thinking skills, especially when you invite your kids to share their ideas. Another is problem-solving in the family, as when you try to come up with different ways to divide up housework or deal with a new puppy that resists house-training.

When your kids have a problem with a friend or sibling, don't give them all the answers. Instead, help them think through various alternative solutions and the outcomes. You could also role-play: What would you do if you're spending the night at your friend's house and she puts on a horror movie that is R-rated? (My daughter Alison encountered this dilemma more than once and had to figure out what to do because scary movies caused bad nightmares for her.)

When riding in the car, brainstorm on how many different ways to use a toothpick, a fork, a plastic foam tray, or the "peanut" packing included in boxes marked "fragile." Asking "What would happen if. . . ?" questions also stimulates creative thinking. Help your child to think about cause and effect. Make it fun dinner conversation. Actually, I think this is how 90 percent of the science-fiction movie scripts are inspired: "What if aliens tried to blow up the earth?" "What if an asteroid was headed right for Washington,

D.C.?" I saw two adventure movies this summer addressing exactly those "what-ifs."

If your kids have to generate ideas for an assignment, suggest a visual way called "clustering." It's a right-brained method that taps the mind for ideas and words, associations and connections. Suggest that your child write the core idea in a circle in the middle of a page. Then, with lines going out like the spokes of a wheel, he quickly writes down around the circle the ideas, feelings, words, phrases, and anything else he can think of that's related to the topic. While he's doing the clustering, don't stop the flow of creativity by saying, "No use writing that word down; it won't work." If you're positive and encouraging, you'll find that lots more ideas will come out of a short time of clustering than by merely listing thoughts in a linear way on the page.

In any problem-solving or thinking activity, when your children do offer a creative solution or different answer than you've thought of, accept and value their ideas. A simple question can be a great stimulator of imaginative thinking. Amy Nappa, author of *Imagine That! 365 Wacky Ways to Build a Creative Christian Family* and a very imaginative mom herself, remembers a time her father greatly encouraged her creativity.

"Amy, I can find two ways to make a square out of these pieces of paper. Could you think of a third way?" he asked.

Impressed that her dad thought she was creative enough to come up with an idea that he hadn't thought of, Amy was not only encouraged to try but to pursue other creative outlets.[8]

Start when your child is young, then keep talking, and you'll be enhancing creative and critical thinking skills—all the while stimulating your child's brain in the Creativity Window of opportunity and having fun together.

Creativity Window Closers to Avoid

Avoid directing your child's play. As my friend Connie Baker, mom of three, says, "Provide materials, close your mouth, and get out of the way" instead of hovering like a helicopter. When Connie served in a children's hospital as a play therapist, she learned if she gave a child art materials, dolls, or medical equipment and encouraged him to "just do it" instead of being "Camp Director" who instructed, "Play this. . .draw this. . .color this purple," the child became much more involved, interested, and expressed feelings and ideas more creatively than when there was a lot of adult interference in the play.

If a child needed assistance, she helped. Otherwise she became "invisible." The point is, avoid putting your agenda for the creative moment on your child. Let him explore, discover, pretend, or make whatever his imagination dreams up.

Let kids have a place where they can get out their stuff and make a mess. Creating can be messy, and if there's never any space where it's OK to mess up or spread out the raw materials, there will be little creative development. When kids have a place for their art or creativity materials, their potential blooms.

Mary Englebreit is a good example. When at nine years old she decided she wanted to be an artist, she announced, "Mommy, I need a studio."

Instead of saying, "We don't have room for an art studio!" her mom emptied the linen closet and put in Mary's desk, chair, pen-and-ink set, and other art materials.[9] It was a tight squeeze, but that closet was where for hours she practiced the skills that have made her one of the most successful greeting card artists in America. Without formal training and with her share of setbacks, Mary carved out a niche for her creativity.

Don't critique or evaluate your child's creations. It's encouragement that fuels creativity, but we throw cold water on the creative spirit with comments like, "No, this isn't the way you draw a dog" or "That's not the right way to do this." Create an attitude of acceptance and encouragement by saying, when your child has a zany idea, "Try it; see how that works." Or you could comment on specific aspects of your child's art (like shapes or colors) or invention (like his originality). Ask a question about how he did the drawing or building rather than asking what it's supposed to be. And don't encourage competition or comparison between different kids' creations.

Allow children to make mistakes and break rules. Albert Einstein said, "A person who never made a mistake never tried anything new." And yes—occasionally break the rules! That may sound radical if you're extremely rule-oriented, but the truth is, always having to go by the rules (like "We don't color people green") puts limits on creative thinking.

"There are certain rules outside of safety rules that children need to have the freedom to break. Nothing new would be invented if some rules weren't broken," says *Imagine That!* author Amy Nappa. Accepting unique and different ways to do something could be the start of your child's creative journey—and your own.

Tapping Into Your Child's Areas of Creative Excitement

One of the reasons it's so important to follow your child's lead and show interest in what she's excited about has to do with the development of creativity. Remember that creativity seems to wane in most kids after the preschool and kindergarten years. It doesn't just decrease because staying in lines is encouraged more than original drawing, or because we overschedule kids, or because we sit them for hours in rows of desks to do structured worksheets in somewhat of a cookie-cutter fashion (although these all contribute to the demise of creativity). It also decreases because of what's happening in the child's mind.

The free-spirited, fantasy thinking of preschoolers begins to give way by age six to more logical thought. As this shift begins, it's an important time to tap into a child's own individual interests. Let your child have a say in what to pursue. If your child is interested in and enjoys drawing, art supplies or eventually lessons may be in order; if it's horses or sports, involve them in that. Let your child choose the musical instrument he wants to play. Remember, they're young and don't yet know what they are gifted or talented at, so allow for stops and starts, and don't insist they become little professionals. Give kids the freedom to experiment and explore what they're interested in. It can be a key to an area in which creativity will express itself!

For example, after a night of stargazing, your child is asking tons of questions about the constellations. You could pick up a book at the library about astronomy, the planets, or space travel; visit a planetarium; or get a constellation map to use on future stargazing adventures. Or if your child tells lots of fantasy stories, write some of them down and turn them into books. As his interest grows, encourage him to start a neighborhood or family newsletter or show him how to send his best poem to a magazine. If your child is interested in drama and has a flair for acting, start a drama troupe in your church or community to give opportunities for your child and others.

Your home is the place creativity is born and the best place for it to be nurtured. As you make room for individuality, imaginative thinking, play, problem-solving, and even messes, add generous doses of appreciation, encouragement, and the attitude that it's OK to make mistakes. You'll be keeping open this precious window of opportunity in your child's life and paving the way for a lifetime of creative thinking.

Creativity Boosters and Inexpensive Resources

Photo fun. Provide an inexpensive camera, even a disposable one, for your child to take photos. After developing the film, use the photos to talk about color, design, angles of objects. Then make and decorate albums to store the photos.

Make a mural. Get out crayons and markers, roll out wallpaper (samples are usually free at wallpaper stores), and let kids create their own murals and scenes of dinosaurs or funny people.

Create new games and holidays. Instead of just using store-bought board games, let your child make his own. With a game board made from poster board or cardboard using markers, some pieces for moving around the board, and a dice or spinner, your child can have hours of fun, first creating the game and then playing. Let your child make up a new holiday and celebrate it together.

Use homemade play dough to make creatures. Combine 2 cups flour, 1 cup salt, -3/4 cup water, 2 tablespoons cooking oil, and a few drops of food coloring. Store the dough in a sealable plastic bag and refrigerate when not being used to make creatures, Christmas ornaments, or whatever else your children dream up. Air dry the creations or dry them in a 250-degree oven for 1-1/2 to 2 hours, then paint with acryiic paints.

Try bubble-blowing blasts. Mix liquid dishwashing soap and a spoonful of glycerin. Let your child blow bubbles in all kinds of different shapes, using a straw, a six-pack plastic top, a colander.

Make paper-bag puppets. Start with a paper bag and glue on buttons for eyes and nose, yarn for hair, and trim made from feathers, sequins, buttons, and scraps of fabric. White glue works best. Put up a tension rod in a doorway, hang a pretty curtain, and presto—an easy-to-make theater for puppet plays presented by the children. To complete the make-believe, the children can make their own programs and tickets. Your children will have a ball.

Make a "genius kit." Give each child a bag filled with 10 to 20 of the same objects (pencils, toothpicks, teaspoons, spools—any household items). Using only these objects, each child designs something that can be used for a purpose, such as a hammer, a measuring stick, a broom.

Dress up. Fill a box with dress-up clothes, costumes, props, hats—whatever treasures your attic holds. Your kids can spend hours pretending.

Check out art museums and community art centers. Visit places where your child can see the paintings of the old masters or take pottery, watercolor, or sculpture classes. Or put on your own art classes at home with art supplies, collage materials, easel, and fabric.

Heavenly Father, Author, and Creator of everything
—from the highest mountains to the smallest kittens,
koalas, flamingos, blue lightning, multicolored rainbows,
and our precious children—
and Giver of every good and perfect gift,
Thank you for the gift of creativity in my child.
Help me to nurture that creative spark,
to fan the flame in all kinds of fun ways instead of blowing it out.
Stir up my own creativity
and remind me to always give you the credit and glory.

Four

---

the curiosity window

A stranger to our planet, every normal child is born curious.
He interacts freely with what he discovers around him, unen-
cumbered by set ideas. He manipulates, experiments, and
explores. The child whose curiosity is accepted as valid is
given the green light to learn. [1]

DOROTHY CORKILLE BRIGGS

"Why don't we have wheels instead of feet?"

"How many skies are there, Mommy?"

"Where does the light go when you turn off that switch?"

"Why does that cloud look like a big ship?"

Constant questions like these characterize the "Curiosity Window," that marvelous time that starts at birth and continues throughout the growing-up years when kids are asking questions, pondering mysteries, and exploring and investigating their environment.

The Curiosity Window begins as soon as babies enter the world. Infants have a passion for discovering and learning. To make sense of their surroundings and to respond to people and events around them, babies start that miraculous process of exploring all the sights, sounds, and information swirling around them. One educator described a baby as a shopper staring at the myriad of merchandise in the windows of a fabulous new department store, waiting for the doors to open.

By the time that little baby is walking—or running—around your house, he can finally reach out and touch those colorful objects he's been gazing at from Mom's arms or from his bouncy chair, and he wants to feel everything—then quickly put it in his mouth. Crawlers and toddlers explore, investigate, dump out cupboard drawers, imitate and entertain like stand-up comedians, and chase butterflies as they move from flower to flower. These eager learners have a natural curiosity about their environment that we can either nurture or throw cold water on.

Often their investigations can be messy, irritating, or cause us adults to be late. Sometimes they seem to be a waste of time or can even be dangerous—like the time our curious two-and-a-half-year-old Chris grabbed a handful of poisonous mushrooms out of a neighbor's yard on one of our nature walks around the block and stuffed them in his little mouth (syrup of ipecac took care of that and out came the mushrooms). So we wonder—is fostering their curiosity important and is it worth the trouble?

The answer is "Yes!" Nurturing your child's curiosity by stimulating and encouraging wonder during this window of opportunity is one of the most important things you can do in the early years and throughout your child's life. It's even more valuable than spending lots of money on specially designed learning toys.

In fact, curiosity makes the brain grow. Curiosity is the most powerful stimulus to building the connections between neurons, or brain cells, that increases the brain's capacity. In the first three years of life, literally trillions of connections are formed between neurons. Curiosity is the catalyst for these natural little scientists to investigate, explore, touch, taste, manipulate and take apart, and pull the cat's tail to see what happens. Curiosity spurs the tons of "why" questions they ask. As long as children stay curious, they tend to be motivated learners. But when curiosity dies, much of the motivation for problem-solving and learning wanes.

Many experts say curiosity may be the most important factor for children's brain development and success in reading, writing, science, and the many academic tasks they face at school. Schools and the business community rank a person's ability to question and problem-solve as even more important to success and achievement than memorizing and retrieving information by rote.

"The years between two and seven seem to be crucial in how children deal with the mysteries," says Gloria Latham, an early childhood professor from Australia. "Within these years they form beliefs, biases, artistry, curiosity, and a sense of self that carries them forward and into adulthood."[2]

If encouraged and given plenty of opportunities for questioning and active exploration, all children can be curious thinkers and remain so throughout their lives.

"In fact," says Dr. Jane Healy, author of *How to Have Intelligent and Creative Conversations with Your Kids*, "we've learned recently that your brain can continue to grow even into old age if you can manage to stay curious, try new things, and have new and interesting experiences."[3]

What We Know: What Happens to Curiosity

If curiosity is such an important link to learning, why does it seem to decline every year as kids grow? Since that decline starts in the early years, let's look for a moment at what happens when children's curiosity gets snuffed out.

Picture a kindergarten class. The teacher asks a few questions and ten little hands wave in the air. "Pick me! I know that!" they call. Then hands go back up as the kids turn the tables, asking the teacher questions. Now picture a seventh grade class. When the teacher asks a question, how many hands wave eagerly? Very few!

Research, including studies by Dr. James Dillon of the University of California, shows that as kids get older, their innate curiosity seems to wane. By the time they reach middle school, many students don't see the classroom as a wonder-filled place where they can't wait to learn something new. Even worse, by the time they get to ninth grade, they ask few questions beyond "How long 'til lunch?" or "When do we get outta here?" In studies of fifty-five high school classrooms, during an entire school day, Dillon found *only eleven* out of eight hundred students asked real questions that solicited learning information. What happened to all that inquisitiveness?

Some experts say the decrease in curiosity is partially due to development.[4] Remember that "free-thinking" or "magical-thinking" approach to life that preschoolers are gifted with temporarily? Without rules binding their thinking, they ponder endless questions like "Why does a ladybug fly away?" or "Can I fly?" By the time they're about six, kids are more concrete and logical in their thinking. Their inquisitiveness becomes more focused and thoughtful. Their curiosity begins to reflect their own individual interests.

But their curiosity doesn't have to decrease. Parents can take an active, positive role in encouraging and promoting curiosity in their children. Even with the natural developmental changes that occur, curiosity can be enhanced. Here's how.

What You Can Do to Enhance Curiosity

Create a Wonder-Filled Place for Play and Exploration

Childproof your house by removing dangerous objects so you can allow your child to play with simple household objects and kitchen gadgets. Set aside a little table in the kitchen as your child's space—with a bright-colored plastic tote for containers with lift-off tops. Inside the containers put objects of different textures and shapes, art supplies, puzzles to put together, and other interesting things.

Having firm, loving limits and providing boundaries at home are important, but a constant barrage of "no" every time kids try to explore or figure things out dampens their inborn desire to find out how things work and why. Reserve your "no" for safety and other vital issues while you make a place and time for both indoor and outdoor play and exploration.

Take your children on excursions and field trips to fascinating places that engage their attention and offer new experiences—a working farm, a hands-on science museum, a zoo, parks, nature trails, and of course your own backyard. Even the grocery store can be an interesting place for a toddler—seeing the red lobsters in the fish market tank and the variety of shapes and colors in fruits and vegetables. Kids need time to look at the stars, watch humming-birds, study rainstorms as they move closer, and experience wonder at the marvels of creation *firsthand* rather than just reading about them. Even in middle school and high school, students need challenging experiments and projects to keep them interested and motivated.

Handle Questions with Enthusiasm and Interest

As soon as your child talks, he begins to ask questions—hundreds of them. By the time he's three or four years old, he wonders about everything. "Why is my tongue pink?" "Why can't I fly?" "Why is the snow cold?" "Why does our cat have whiskers?" "Why don't we drink milk like our cat does?" At first the questions are considered cute, but when there's a constant stream of them and parents are busy and over-scheduled, parents respond less than enthusiastically. The following can help to spark a child's curiosity.

Don't feel like you have to have all the answers. Remember, it's better to know some of the questions than to have all the answers. Often children don't want answers from adults, they just want to see if we're interested and listening. Asking kids for their own answers or solutions encourages kids to ask more questions. Help your child to think through a question and deduce possible solutions. If your child asks how all of a sudden the green leaves turned red, you could respond, "What do *you* think about how the leaves got so red and golden?" Or "How do *you* think the cat got his whiskers?" if that's what he's puzzled about.

If you don't know an answer and your child really wants to know, write the question on an index card (keep a stack handy on your kitchen counter and in your car), and the next time you're near the library together, go in and search for an answer. You'll be giving your child a powerful demonstration of how to conduct an inquiry, and it won't cost but a few pennies for the cards.

Kids have great potential for creative thinking. Often they use stories and complex theories to explain things. Here's a five-year-old's explanation of how our brains work:

Your brain listens to your thoughts and if your thoughts are wrong, your mouth tells you. The mouth can have an argument with the brain. Sometimes our brain gets very tired of thinking and gets a headache. Then it can't think of a thing. That's a problem. It's like the light bulb went out.[5]

Respecting our children's ideas and thoughts when they explain things can make a big difference. Here's what Darrel Baumgardner, a cloud physicist at the National Weather Center in Colorado, told me about how his parents' influence impacted his curiosity: "I've always been curious and, more importantly, a risk taker when it came to learning about new things or launching into new directions of study. Had I been ridiculed as a child for coming up with the 'wrong' answer, I might have been different. I was fortunate, however, to have parents who encouraged my reading in a broad range of subjects and supported me in whatever questioning or endeavor I took an interest. They still do today!"[6]

The questioning process can continue all through childhood and into adulthood if, especially in the middle school and high school years, we are careful not to put children down for their different, or "off-the-wall," ideas and answers. A young person's fear of "looking dumb" because of an answer can stifle inquisitiveness.

Let your child hear you asking questions aloud of yourself and other people. When you're alone with your child, rather than always directing questions to her, make an observation followed by a question like, "Wow, look at the color of that sunset tonight! I wonder why it's more red tonight than last night?" Or use mind-stretching "what if" questions. Einstein said that playing around with "what if" questions in his mind was how he came up with some of his best discoveries, so you're in good company when you ask them. Use research-type questions like "What do we need to know to make this birdhouse?" And problem-solving questions like "What are you going to do about the conflict between you and your friend? What are three ways you could solve it?" Then, if your child shows interest, follow with a dialogue of mutual information-gathering or brainstorming rather than a quiz.

Asking interesting and fun questions at the dinner table (questions that don't always have a right answer) also boosts curiosity and thinking. Questions like "Try to imagine what your life would be like if you were our cat. What things could you do that you can't do now and what couldn't you do?"[7]

Be Observant

Point out the crocuses coming up in the spring; talk about the cycles of nature; ponder out loud your wonderings about the world around you. In that way, you're modeling curiosity and keeping your own sense of wonder alive. And, in the process, your child may become interested and want to know more.

Provide "tinkering time." Lots of kids today are so over-scheduled they run from one after-school sport to another and have almost no time to just play in the backyard or pursue a fascination. Yet in a landmark study of the early lives of 400 eminent adults—inventors, artists, explorers, great statesmen—to find common elements that led to their later achievements, one major factor was found: as children they had been encouraged and allowed time to "tinker" and playfully explore their interests and the world around them. As kids they were given freedom to make messes, make choices, and do different things than their peers.[8] Providing materials and tinkering time instead of one more structured activity might be one of the best things you could give your child.

Read Aloud to Your Children

Pick topics that your child is most interested in. Although reading has many benefits for language development, it's also a great curiosity booster. Seeing pictures of whales and sea creatures, jet planes and faraway places stimulates thinking and imagination. Books can take children to places they can't go, and explain mysteries and marvels of nature.

Provide Tools of Discovery

Simple objects, like a magnifying glass, a telescope, a microscope, even a paper towel tube to take a closer look at what's hiding in the grass, can stimulate your child's curiosity. With these simple materials, a walk in the woods can become an adventure in exploration. Bring along a small garden trowel and a sturdy shoe box for carrying home rocks, pieces of plants, pine cones, and small animal bones.

Be Involved

"The growth of our intelligence comes from spontaneous emotional interaction with others—and best of all, parents," says Dr. Stanley Greenspan, author of *The Growth of the Mind*. He advises that the key thing to do with preschoolers is to get down on the floor and involve yourself in pretend play. Don't simply read to your five-year-old. Read a few paragraphs and have your child finish the story. In the school years, foster curiosity by eliciting your child's opinions and debating one side. Make up stories together. Invite your child's different ideas. Greenspan says, "These are the vibrant emotional interactions between child and parent that give rise to the child's ability to wonder and think up new ideas," and they are the best brain boosters of all.[9]

Teachable moments for these spontaneous interactions are all around us, some right in our own backyards. When my friend Sally and her family moved to the Tallahassee, Florida, area, they heard that the lake on their property held a resident alligator—an eight-foot-long alligator who was most attracted to dogs and children. The more they heard, the more fascinated their eight children became.

Sally decided to capitalize on their curiosity, so parents and children engaged in some investigation. They got books from the library on alligators, information on the Internet, and interviewed neighbors. The kids drew pictures of what they thought their neighborhood alligator looked like and, with their parents, watched the water, hoping to see it. The first time the alligator rose up out of the water, eyes looking straight at them, the children could hardly believe what they saw. The creature was *ten* feet long, not eight!

Soon after, the local wildlife agency took the alligator to a wildlife preserve. The children continued to be observant of their new environment, finding raccoons, possums, egrets, blue herons, and other creatures to investigate.

One dad I know took his kids to a greenhouse and plant nursery. They watched the potting of plants and saw many different varieties of flowers, plants, and trees. They saw how the nurseryman controls pests and plant diseases. They went home and planted seedlings in paper cups and egg cartons to make their own indoor garden. They took a magnifying glass to the city rose garden and looked at all the different colors and sizes of hybrid roses, talking about the great variety of beautiful things God created for us to enjoy. In the process, this father stirred up a lifelong love of green plants, flowers, and discovery in his daughters.

Encourage Kitchen Questions

The kitchen is another place for spontaneous interactions between you and your child that stir inquisitiveness. If your child wonders aloud about what would happen if he mixes water and cooking oil, let him try it and discuss what happens. Use cooking to demonstrate that substances change when mixed, heated, or frozen. While preparing meals, in addition to stirring up some good food, try to stir your child's thinking with questions like: Why does bread rise? Why do you think the cookies turn brown in the oven? Why should we wash our hands before making food? How can you tell from the bedroom when I'm cooking pizza? If you're blindfolded, does the peanut butter sandwich taste as good? And then try it.

Choose Schools That Encourage Curiosity

Be selective about the kind of learning environment you choose for your child. Some schools have a positive, motivating effect on students' curiosity and desire to learn. Others have a negative effect. Visiting classrooms and being involved is the best way to find out whether your child's classroom is an enriching environment with a big range of resources that encourages real learning and discovery.

Whether your child is in a public or private school or is home-schooled, gather with other parents and take an active role in getting a creative, stimulating kind of environment for the children.

Using all their senses, children in the Curiosity Window years between birth and age five begin to form ideas about how things work. They start to make sense of their surroundings. They develop security and confidence as they wonder, discover, and gain knowledge for themselves. All this concrete learning is a vital foundation for later abstract, symbolic pencil-and-paper learning from books in school.

With a rich storehouse of experiences gained in childhood— interesting sights and sounds, people and places visited, time to observe and play and talk and explore—your child's curiosity will stay alive and well throughout the growing-up years and way beyond, in fact throughout a lifetime.

Curiosity Window Closers to Avoid

Avoid curriculum-driven, memorization-focused class-rooms in the early years. Research shows students in elementary schools do about a thousand worksheets a year,[10] which does little to stimulate most kids' curiosity. The fact is lots of us learned much of what we needed to learn in kindergarten—where there were plenty of hands-on activities like painting, working with clay, creating and manipulating things, and drawing.

However, when kids move on to the elementary grades, they have too many worksheets and too few hands-on activities, which leads to burnout. Children's curiosity and brain development is stimulated by exploring things firsthand. Even in middle school and high school, students need

TIP: Doing an experiment with magnets instead of reading about magnetism and counting real pennies rather than coloring pennies in a workbook are hands-on activities that stimulate a child's curiosity.

challenging experiments and projects to keep them interested and motivated. Work with your child's school to provide a varied curriculum and more hands-on learning opportunities in science.

Resist the urge to overprotect, do, or demonstrate everything for your child. Overprotection squelches curiosity. So does performing for a child all the tasks that seem difficult. It's tempting to put the shapes and balls in the shape sorter if your toddler is frustrated with them (and later give all the answers to his homework when he's struggling). But it's better to say something like, "I guess this square doesn't fit in this round hole. What about this hole? Why don't you try it?" Then encourage your child to persevere. Give plenty of opportunities for a child to figure things out and make mistakes without being scolded—mistakes are the stuff science discoveries are made of! Let your children handle things they can handle safely. Let them mix ingredients in the kitchen (with supervision, of course) to see what happens.

If your child doesn't understand a math problem, instead of giving the answer, provide manipulatives like small blocks, miniature cars, or even edible counters like raisins or mini-marshmallows to touch and handle to see why $5 + 8 = 13$.

Accept your child's out-of-the-box, creative answers and hypotheses. Even if you can see some holes in the thinking, instead of correcting or criticizing, have your child talk the idea through and then ask for more information.

Avoid choosing everything for your child. Instead, offer him choices. If hobbies, lessons, sports, and after-school activities are always chosen by parents and driven by adult motivation, your child will have little opportunity to find out what he's curious about and interested in. Encourage him to dream about what he'd most like to do, talk about what pushes his "interest" buttons, then pursue those things.

Give materials that encourage flexible thinking and motivate kids to risk using different strategies for solving problems: paper and crayons as opposed to coloring books, discovery toys and things children can create and build with, items to use to explore the wonders of nature. Studies have shown that kids who have played with blocks, construction toys, and puzzles are more motivated to search for a variety of solutions than are children whose experiences have been mostly with structured, adult-directed lessons and play and thus use a rigid single strategy to solve problems.

Resources for Developing Curiosity

Science kits like a frog hatchery, ant or ladybug farms, and a butterfly nursery can be purchased at learning stores and some toy stores.

Make your own magnet kit by putting a big magnet in a sealable plastic bag with a tiny metal car, a cookie cutter, and other metal things to use in experiments.

Microscopes, chemistry sets, and other science tools encourage curiosity, but the backyard, garage, and kitchen are also good labs to learn in. Do experiments like balloon mysteries, where you get a handful of balloons of different sizes and shapes. Blow the balloons up and let them go, one at a time. Let your child make observations, such as how far each goes, whether the flight was straight or erratic, and how long each stayed in the air. Then ponder why the big balloon didn't go as far as the little one and other cause-and-effect phenomena of the balloon launch. Mix oil and water and watch them separate. Or blow bubbles using soap and glycerin to demonstrate viscosity.

Keep a backpack handy for exploring. Inside the backpack put a magnifying glass, a "critter jar" (plastic container fitted with a mesh lid to let in air), old plastic tubs with snap tops for storing "treasures" found along the way, and a sturdy old spoon for digging.

Make a backyard bird habitat with your child. Investigate (by checking with your county agriculture agent or by reading books) the kind of habitat birds in your area like. Then plan a healthy habitat. Let your child help decide where to put the bird feeder, bird bath, or bird house in your yard. Then make one or all of the items. These can be simple rectangular wooden bird houses or a pine cone rolled first in peanut butter and then in birdseed, or a clear liter-size soft-drink bottle with a window cut into the side for birds to eat from, hung on a tree limb. Then get a bird guidebook and have fun learning!

For a birthday or Christmas, give a book or a subscription to a science magazine. In addition, watch science programs on the Discovery and PBS channels and discuss what you learned. Take outings to hands-on science museums that feature educational displays designed especially for kids to touch.

Lord of all, you have designed and prewired my child's curiosity,
her interested, enthusiastic questioning about her world.
As much as you have patience with me,
give me patience with my child when she asks "Why?" for the tenth time!
Help me to enjoy this window of wonder
that's so fleeting.
Keep me curious and interested in the world too!

Five

the physical window

Children are like clocks;
they must be allowed to run! [1]

JAMES C. DOBSON

At eight and a half months, Caitlin turns over to her tummy and reaches for the pink Beanie Baby bunny. Gotcha! She looks over the stuffed rabbit, chews on the label for less than a minute, and then peers over her shoulder to the toys on her right a few feet away. No problem. She rotates her spine and quickly shifts her weight far enough to the right to flip over again and again until she's within reach of the desired bright-colored plastic keys. She turns her prize over in her hands, chews on it, and shakes it to hear the clacking sound it makes.

Rolling over again, a big smile lights Caitlin's face as she grabs hold of a velvety green frog—which she promptly sticks in her mouth, amused by the squeaky sound it makes when squeezed and chewed. After a few minutes, she throws the frog across the room (Caitlin has a very good right arm; we think she may develop into quite a pitcher). Scooting over to the toy basket, she tips it on its side and starts "tasting" the toys inside to see what feels interesting. After testing a few, she picks a blue plastic baby doll to accompany her on another rolling excursion, this time across the living room floor.

I turn my head for a moment and all of a sudden Caitlin has transformed her position from lying down to sitting, giggling at her new-found skill. She playfully pitches the tiny baby doll in front of her as if to give herself a challenge. She reaches for it with all her might, almost in a crawling position, but not quite sure how to get those hips and legs to cooperate. So she turns, turns again, reaching to the right until she has rotated almost 360 degrees from where she started. Unable to get the doll, Caitlin changes her gaze to the stacking toy in front of her and promptly dismantles it, watching as the orange circle rolls across the floor. The wheels of the mind are turning and Caitlin is doing some important "problem-solving." She wants to move to the toy, about five feet away, but alas, she can't figure out how—at least not today. Instead, she kicks her feet and busies herself with a small rubber giraffe.

Naturally, as a grandma, I watch these movements with delight. It wasn't too long ago that I remember this same grandbaby being brought home from the Neonatal Intensive Care Unit looking like a miniature in the yellow and blue car seat her parents carried her in. We had all breathed a sigh of relief and many thanks to God when Caitlin, after being a month premature and in critical condition, was well enough to move from the NICU to her own nursery.

Once home, Caitlin in the early weeks was mainly interested in nursing and in being cuddled by her mom and dad. As with most infants, her movements were directed by reflexes rather than intention. When Tiffany stroked her on her cheek, Caitlin turned her head toward Mom's hand, looking for food. She responded to her mom's voice and especially her singing. When lying on her back with her head turned to one side, the arm on the same side straightened as her opposite arm bent (called the tonic neck reflex). When startled at a sudden, sharp noise, Caitlin threw her arms and legs out and cried, yet she could sleep through the dull roar of the dryer or a television program.

I remember the first time I saw her smile her magical smile. Her first time to reach for the toy in the mobile over her head. The day she sat up for the first time. Her preliminary attempts at rolling over. Every little milestone of development was a wonder to me, but then I've always been fascinated by how babies learn and grow.

What We Know: Healthy Physical Development

From birth through age two, we know that most children learn to grasp, sit up, crawl, stand, and walk. By age three to five, they master motor skills that require coordination—like hopping, skipping, throwing a ball, climbing, and running. Through play, they explore space and objects around them, and thrill parents and grandparents with every milestone reached, every skill gained.

While I'm not going to take you on a month-by-month tour of your child's motor development (there are numerous good books on the subject), we do want to look at some new understandings about the "Physical Window" and how we can promote and support children's growth in the area of motor coordination.[2]

The Beginnings of Movement

Motor development doesn't begin at birth; it began in utero, when at seven weeks the preborn infant's movements began. Movement peaks between the fifteenth and seventeenth weeks. This is the time when the areas of the brain controlling movement start to be "wired," or connected. From this point, it takes approximately two years for cells in the cerebellum (the part of the brain that controls posture, movement, balance, and coordination) to form functioning circuits.[3]

Time Span for Physical Development

The most critical part of the Physical Window lasts approximately four years, or until the fifth birthday. Although there is improved eye-hand coordination, increased strength and dexterity, and motor development during all the growing-up years, the first four years are crucial. We know this partly because of the effect of restricting movement: for example, a child unable to move for the first four years due to being restricted in a body cast until age four or five will eventually learn to walk, but not with the ease or smoothness of a child who had full range of movement in the first few years.[4]

There are critical periods during which experience is essential for motor development. Motor skills such as sitting up, crawling, standing, and walking develop only if the baby is exposed to relevant sensory stimuli during the prime time of the window of opportunity. While most parents wouldn't intentionally deprive their child, sometimes infants lack the stimulation of being on the floor or they don't have interaction of parents in play. A baby needs the experience of learning how to move, the stimulation of being on the floor—both on the tummy and the back—of feeling movement through the body. Without this experience, children may not move out and explore their environment and develop curiosity, which can lead to delays in cognitive abilities—their perception, reasoning, and thinking skills.

Sensory Stimuli

Baby's movements are guided by sensory input such as vision, hearing, touch, taste, smell, and the perception of movement coming from the environment or from the baby's own body. All the sensory systems provide important information to the child in the process of learning movement. If a baby is often confined in a car seat and baby seats (like bouncy chairs, swings, Johnny-Jump-Ups, stationary walkers) and hasn't had the opportunity to get out and move and experience what her body does when she plays on the floor, then she may not be stimulated and motivated to move.

For example, four-month-old Marissa was such an irritable baby, her mom entertained her in a swing, infant seat, car seat, or on her lap. But Marissa didn't seem to be developing certain motor skills. After talking with Marissa's doctor about her concerns, Marissa's mom began to put Marissa on her tummy with two favorite toys. She would put a mirror in front of Marissa to stimulate her to push up on her forearms and stay up so she could "see the baby." In this way, Marissa was building endurance for this and other activities. Then she began to reach for toys to one side. She began to explore, to touch, and look—her curiosity was moving her on!

A Progression from Head to Foot

Babies begin to develop the head control and trunk control needed for sitting, the control of the hips needed for crawling, culminating with the control of the knees and ankles they need for walking. Carlton, playing on his tummy, first learned head control in all positions as he began to work simultaneously on strengthening his back muscles. When lying on his back, he often reached for toys or kicked at them with his legs bent toward his chest, doing his first "crunches" and strengthening his "abs," or tummy muscles. By seven months, he was able to stabilize his head and trunk to sit up.

Let's go back to the bouncy chair or stationary walker—if a baby is put in these devices too early (two to five months) or too often before developing control of its head and trunk, the baby tends to stiffen up to get stability and learns movement patterns that are counterproductive. A stationary walker should be used *only* when a baby has control of head and trunk and only for very short periods of time. When babies spend too much time in upright, supportive seats, they don't gain the benefit of strengthening their muscles through repetition and play that's horizontal (when they are on their backs). Floor play is important for motor development. It requires more effort to move against gravity, which strengthens the muscles.

Further Progress from Proximal to Distal

In regular parent talk, "proximal to distal" means that children gain control of movement at their shoulders that progresses outward to elbows, wrists, hands, and fingers. In order to strengthen the shoulder muscles, babies need to play on their tummies and backs. Floor play, three times a day (morning, afternoon, and evening), is needed for exploring movement.

At first, movement is random. It happens accidentally. Then as the baby

TIP: Your baby will enjoy floor play more if you pick morning times when baby is alert and playful, not right before eating or when tired and ready for bed.

continues to move, he gains valuable information. Through much practice and repetition, the task or movement becomes easier to accomplish as the circuits that connect thinking to motor cortex to nerves that move the muscles get in gear. It's quite a process!

As babies repeat a movement, they begin to make adjustments due to the sensory feedback. After moving and practicing a movement over and over, babies begin to understand how that movement was achieved so they can do it again. In the process, synapses, or connections, are made between nerve cells in the brain until a pattern is established and the brain is "hardwired" for that skill.

New Skills

When a baby is putting a lot of energy and effort into learning a new motor skill, he won't exert as much effort in another area. For example, if your child begins pulling up, standing, and taking steps preliminary to walking, he often becomes quieter and has less verbal interaction during this intensive motor stage. Don't worry; it doesn't mean his language has regressed. It means he's concentrating on a new skill.

The Importance of Touch

Touch is extremely important to the development of healthy children. For babies and young children, physical touch in the form of hugs, snuggling, and cuddling has many benefits: it boosts the immune system, increases bonding and attachment between parent and child, and is an important stimulus to the nervous system and vital for motor development.

The Importance of Play

Play is the work of children. Play entices babies and young children to move repeatedly until they've mastered a new movement. That's where you come in. You are your child's best plaything! In the early months, babies need a goal or motivation for moving, such as reaching for a set of bright plastic keys that Mom is holding out. While a colorful mobile can stimulate interest for short periods of time, eventually your baby will want some human interaction. And just as kids need their parents to talk to them and sing to them, they also need parents to interact with them in ways that stimulate movement. When you squeak the toy or turn on the music, you provide the motivation for movement.

It doesn't take expensive toys to stimulate motor development. Researchers at the University of Alabama found that simple things—blocks and big plastic beads, peekaboo games and other activities parents do naturally with their baby—enhance motor, cognitive, and language development the most.[5] Simple playthings like pots and pans, boxes, plastic kitchenware, dolls, and balls can entertain and stimulate kids for hours.

The learning of new motor, cognitive, and other skills evolves out of a motivating task the child tends to choose to do, says my friend Kay Davis, a pediatric physical therapist who has worked with hundreds of children in motor development. "Children will show us how to teach them if we follow their lead and challenge their curiosity and learning style. Go with the activity that's interesting to them," she says. Then tailor the learning task or skill to that activity.

For example, when Kay's sons Ross and Blake were preschoolers, Ross was more motor driven and tactile, or touch, oriented. If she wanted to work on number concepts with Ross, he learned much more if they counted trucks as he pushed them through the sand in his sandbox. He'd touch and feel the trucks, and there was movement involved. Her older son Blake enjoyed the little workbooks she purchased. He liked to sit and think and was visually stimulated. He could entertain himself at a desk and figure out number concepts just by looking at a page in the workbook. The secret was in finding what was stimulating and interesting to each child.

What You Can Do: Providing Opportunity

Birth to six months: Unbreakable crib mirrors stimulate a baby with an ever-changing view with each arm or leg movement. Music tapes and music boxes are pleasurable for infants. Between two and four months, babies begin to bat and swipe at toys, and then gain enough control of their arms and hands to grasp and manipulate objects. To practice this movement, mobiles (if low enough for baby to bat at the objects) are fun, and crib gyms or toy bars (a frame with suspended rattles, links, or objects) offer reaching and grabbing activities. Tummy play is important so baby can put weight on forearms. Put baby on her back and play bicycle, gently rotating her legs, playing peekaboo, or holding out a toy for her to reach for.

Six to nine months: Most babies are working on sitting during this time frame. You can put toys on top of a footstool, low bench, or stacked couch pillows so the toys are a little higher off the floor (directly in front or to the side) where baby has to reach to get them. Provide a variety of interesting textures to feel (soft, hard, rough, smooth). For exploration, use large colorful balls, puzzles with knobs, board books, bath toys for dunking, and safe places to crawl where the premises have been "babyproofed" beforehand.

Nine to eighteen months: Babies may want to practice climbing, and an "obstacle course" gives them a reason and improves coordination. Big floor pillows with toys on them or an egg crate pillow (big chunks of foam egg crate sewn inside sheeting material) are safe "obstacles." They will love to climb on these and will have to work a little harder to maneuver—pulling with arms, pushing with legs. Boxes to climb into (if on their side), like big refrigerator cartons, offer baby a place to crawl in and explore. A tablecloth over a card table where they can crawl in and peek out is also fun and stimulating. They can practice kicking with balls, playing with toys with levers, and playing with blocks that can be pushed through different-size slots (shape sorters).

Eighteen months to two years: All the playground equipment you can provide in a safe, fenced yard—such as swing and slide—are challenging and fun. Look for play lawn mowers and other push toys, rocking horses and rocking chairs, climbing structures, "busy boxes," blocks, and pegboards. Toys for nesting, pounding, screwing, digging, and stringing are stimulating and develop motor skills. Check garage sales for good buys on all indoor and outdoor toys.

Three to six years: Tricycles (with helmet) and other riding toys, playground equipment, and sandboxes stocked with plastic trucks and animals all motivate preschoolers to move and to gain motor skills.

In toddler and preschool years, fine motor skills can be encouraged with an arts-and-crafts hour at home using safe children's scissors, colored pencils, crayons, stickers, clay, or homemade play dough. Encourage your child to throw balls into a basket or container to improve coordination and aim. Practice balance by walking on a homemade balance beam (make with cement blocks and a sturdy board), walking on tiptoe, or curb walking.

Games like "Follow the Leader" and "Simon Says" encourage imitative play. "Hide-and-seek" always engages kids' curiosity. Encourage play with blocks, windup toys, and large beads (much too big to be swallowed).

Also, provide indoor exercisers for rainy or extra-cold days—like Nerf basketballs and goals, chinning bars that fit in a doorway and can be adjusted to a child's height, construction equipment like LEGOs or blocks of different sizes, and heavy plastic play equipment.

Don't forget that even though purchased toys are great and your child will likely enjoy certain ones, there's also a tremendous amount of stimulation from ordinary household objects such as plastic containers and lids, pots and pans to bang together, and cardboard boxes to play with and in.

Restricting the amount of time preschoolers watch TV and play Nintendo or video games will aid their motor development. While they may be entertained by TV and Nintendo, these aren't as interactive as playing outside, riding a Big Wheel, or climbing on a geodesic dome, and they don't improve large motor coordination. Although playing video games may seem to give fine motor or eye-hand coordination practice, it's not worth the toll that it takes in other areas—shorter attention span, lack of large motor exercise, and lack of language practice.

Keep Your Child Moving!

Since the average preschooler is like a little Energizer bunny, he tends to get enough exercise to optimize his health if given space and opportunities such as those described above. But every year from fourth grade on, children get more sedentary until activity drops off drastically in the teen years.[6] The twenty-five to fifty hours of television and Nintendo many kids use as "play" or entertainment time is one of the major reasons for the epidemic of overweight and lack of fitness in kids. Exercise habits are developed early—if your child is allowed to be a couch potato, that pattern will likely continue. If she learns to enjoy exercise when she's young, she's very likely to continue being active for a lifetime.

What can you do? Make sure your children get the exercise they need—at least an hour of healthy play every day and several more on the weekend.

Instead of forcing exercise, be a positive role model by being physically active yourself. Make exercise a family affair! Active parents tend to raise active kids. So take the lead and introduce your child to lots of varied activities, always emphasizing fun rather than just competition or winning. Go to the park for a game of tag or to swing, jump rope in the driveway, shoot hoops or throw a baseball, fly a kite, take a nature walk. And allow your kids some unstructured playtime.

When you plan family outings or vacations, make them active—like a trip to a zoo or hiking in a national park. Include swimming, biking, or roller-blading. Even chores like raking leaves, walking the dog, or washing the car on a warm summer day can provide opportunities for physical activity.

Don't expect school to be the only place your child gets physical exercise. The fact is, due to budget cuts and other factors, only a third of children and adolescents ages ten to seventeen participate in a daily physical education program at school.

Help your children find sports they like and are good at—it doesn't have to be a team sport. They could try karate, jogging, bicycling, tennis, hiking, gymnastics, or dance. Aerobic exercise (like walking at a good clip, swimming, bicycling, or aerobic dance) improves the cardiovascular system. Stretching and repetition exercises improve flexibility and muscle tone.

Let your child's interests lead the way, and keep the activity appropriate for his age (like providing your six-year-old a small ball and a basket only six feet high instead of a full-size basketball and a regulation ten-foot basket). Watch what your child is doing after school; if it's vegging out in front of a television set, encourage him to play with a friend or join after-school programs that provide physical activities.

What We Know: The Nutrition Connection

What your child eats affects brain development, learning, and overall health and fitness. Scientists are learning more all the time about the mind-body-food connection. We know that good nutrition supports maximum brain development in all areas, including motor development. All kinds of studies have been done that show good nutrition positively impacts kids' brain function. Recent research from the University of California at Davis, for example, showed that when students came to school well nourished, they performed better on cognitive tests, had improved memory, and improved verbal fluency. On the other hand, when they skipped breakfast, it changed the way the children's brains worked, lowering the speed and accuracy of information retrieval and diminishing school performance.[7]

After your child is off pureed baby foods and onto "people foods," begin to teach good nutrition habits. Kids need calories to grow—lots of them—so don't restrict their diet too much. Just make sure they have more good-for-you foods and fewer high-calorie, low-nutrient, empty junk foods. Take them shopping at the grocery store so they can pick out their favorite nutritious foods and learn how to decipher labels. Don't place pressure on kids to be slim (or they become critical of their bodies, and those negative feelings can last a lifetime). Instead, put the spotlight on good health. Get the whole family involved, and eating well becomes something positive you do together. Provide brain-boosting foods like these:

Complex carbohydrates, such as bagels, whole-wheat bread, oatmeal, vegetables, and fruit, to keep energy up and stimulate serotonin, a brain chemical linked to calmness. Also, the fiber in fruits and whole-grain foods improves the functioning of the gastrointestinal system and prevents many diseases of later life. Most kids don't get nearly enough fiber.

Protein, to boost metabolism and increase catecholamines—brain chemicals associated with alertness. A peanut butter or chicken sandwich or some other protein-packed lunch can help fend off afternoon sluggishness on school days.

Calcium, found in milk, yogurt, and cheese, to build bones and teeth.

"Good fats," especially omega-3 fatty acids found in fish (such as tuna and salmon), walnuts, and green leafy veggies. This supernutrient may improve children's brain function and enhance their ability to focus and concentrate on tasks and learning.

Iron, from red meat, beans, and other foods, for good concentration.

Munchies, such as a variety of fresh fruit in a big basket, dried fruits and nuts, whole-grain crackers, granola or protein bars for quick "pick-me-ups," low-sugar fruit muffins, popcorn, and fruit smoothies.

From the floor play and exercise of your children's first year to a combination of lots of fun, heart-pumping activities and smart, nutritious eating, your children will be on their way to healthy bodies *and minds!*

Physical Window Closers to Avoid

Bombarding baby with too much too soon. Sincere, overzealous moms who want their kids to learn a lot of new skills all at once may try to teach a toddler colors, the alphabet, and potty training all on the same day, an approach that may be counterproductive. New studies show that the brain needs to rest to store new skills. Researchers have found that it takes five to six hours for the memory of a new skill to move from a temporary storage site in the front of the brain to a more long-term, permanent storage site in the back of the brain. "During those six hours, there is a neural 'window of vulnerability' when the new skill can be easily wiped from memory if the person attempts to learn another skill" right on top of the new one.[8] So if your child learns a new piano piece, let her focus on that one thing for the day instead of launching into learning a whole different composition. If the brain gets to rest and store the new piece, it will be retained longer.

Lack of toys. If we think in the first few months of infancy there's not much going on in the brain, baby misses an opportunity for much vital brain stimulation in the motor skills and other areas. Toys don't have to be expensive to be effective and stimulating. Inexpensive toys, household objects, and things a baby can move and manipulate meet the need. Even soft rubber pet toys, which are extremely inexpensive, are very tactile and bright. Because it doesn't take much pressure to make them squeak, they're a good object for making cause-and-effect sound. (Caution: when babies get their teeth, they can bite the toys, so remove these pet toys before that point. Also, some children have latex allergies and many pet toys are made of latex.)

Overstimulating baby. To avoid overstimulating your child with too many toys, put some toys away each week and replace them with other toys. The rotation keeps the toys novel, and that's what babies like—the novelty rather than the super-elaborateness of a toy. Instead of exposing your child to a chaotic array of toys all the time, keep certain toys in certain rooms. Keep others at Grandma's house.

Lack of time. Probably the biggest hindrance to your baby having floor play and interaction with you is lack of time. Setting aside even a little time in the morning, in the afternoon, and in the evening for your child to play on her back and tummy will make a big difference in motor development.

Overprotectiveness. Babies and young children will occasionally fall as they are learning how to move in order to explore, climb, and develop their motor coordination. If they fall in a place where they can safely experience it, the next time they'll figure out a way to correct the problem and not tumble over. In the process, they're doing some important cognitive problem-solving. If young children aren't ever allowed to fall or learn by trial and error, then they don't get important feedback of how to change and improve their movements. For example, a new walker falls a lot but is becoming more proficient in his ability to balance. Soon you'll notice that his arms will be down out of high guard position and he will narrow his base of support, stabilizing his walk. He'll soon be well on his way to being able to run.

Resources for Physical Development

Tent-building and hideaways. Place couch and chairs so that you can suspend a large sheet over them. Inside the tent put a blanket, pillow, flashlight, books and toys, paper and crayons for some inside fun. Or create a hideaway by cutting the bottoms off large cardboard boxes and connecting them to each other with duct tape—to make a tunnel, a house, a climbing place or fort.

Kids' exercise videos. Lively activities set to music, kids' exercise videos are great fun on rainy days.

Scavenger hunt. Make a list of ten things for your children to find around the house (for prereaders, draw pictures of the objects). Then let them set off to find the listed items. For outdoor hunts, try a nature scavenger hunt and list five kinds of leaves, three different-shaped rocks, a feather; or, at the beach, list things they could find by the sea or on the lakeshore.

Instant basketball. Remove the bottom from a big grocery bag and use the rest of the bag as a hoop. Tape the "hoop" to a wall at the right height for your kids, inflate a few balloons, and they're ready for the game to start!

Family outings. Go to a living history farm or museum, a county fair where there are wonderful varieties of animals on display, a zoo or aquarium, art and science museums— anyplace where your kids will be interested in what they can see. Many of these places are close to home. Check with a tourist bureau, historical society, county parks, and recreation departments for information on what your community offers.

Lord, thank you that my child is fearfully and wonderfully made,
that you knit him together in my womb!
Oh, the wonder of your creation and the intricate way
his hands and feet and every part of his body moves and works,
the delight of watching him take first steps, learn and grow,
and explore with delight his surroundings.
Help me to trust you instead of living in fear
and overprotecting my child.
Renew my energy daily so I can keep up with him!

Six

---

the music window

What will a child learn sooner than a song?[1]

ALEXANDER POPE

When Rayma, a mom I know, was pregnant with her daughter, she attended concerts at Florida State University, where her husband was stage manager at Opperman Music Hall. One night Rayma was engrossed in the visual as well as aural delights of a Percussion Ensemble concert. The concert was made forever memorable by the addition of a special participant, their daughter, whose little foot began a perfectly rhythmical accompaniment to the music—the first time her mom had felt her move.

When Robin was expecting her first child, she not only was preparing for the birth but also for her senior vocal performance recital, the last hurdle to obtaining a master's degree in vocal music. Every day during the pregnancy, Robin practiced singing arias and operas. Month by month, baby Annie grew in her womb, surrounded by music for a good portion of her mom's waking hours.

In the first few months after Annie's arrival, Robin made an interesting discovery one day as she was driving across town. Having quickly tired of being in her car seat, Annie began to wail. Her mother tried everything to soothe her—talking quietly to her, turning on a cassette tape of kids' praise, singing a nursery song—but nothing worked. Annie continued to cry. Finally Robin began to sing one of her favorite operas from her senior recital. Immediately the six-week-old baby stopped crying, relaxed, and closed her eyes (as if listening intently). She looked happy.

Annie's enjoyment of opera wasn't a one-time whim; she continued to prefer this style of music throughout her childhood and beyond. Prior to birth, her brain had literally been wired for opera! When Annie learned "Jesus Loves Me," "Old MacDonald," and even "Itsy Bitsy Spider" in her toddler class, she came home singing these play songs in a flamboyant operatic style (which caused a few chuckles from the teacher and the other kids). As a two-year-old she could match pitch and sing whole lines of songs. She went on to master the violin in elementary school.

Our granddaughter, Caitlin, is another good example of how early music has an impact on kids. When only a few weeks old, Caitlin showed a strong preference for certain worship music. When she was fussy and her mom played a Harry Connick or Phish CD, the music had little calming effect. But when her mom played "Holy Is the Lord," Caitlin was immediately soothed. Caitlin's mother, Tiffany, when she was pregnant with Caitlin, was on the worship team at church, surrounding Caitlin with praise and worship music. By the time she was six months old, Caitlin began "singing along" with a "la-la-la-ohh!" kind of unique melody whenever we sang to her.

Experiences such as these go right along with what we're learning from research studies on newborns and young children: kids are much smarter than we think—particularly in the area of music!

Tuning Up the Neurons

When your child learns a play song like "This Old Man" or "Old MacDonald" and chimes in to sing it with other kids, dances in your arms as you listen to a Mozart CD, or is taught to pick out a tune on the piano, what's happening? Much more than we could have imagined before MRIs showed scientists actual pictures of the brain activity of babies and young children. What they've found is that these early musical experiences wire the brain somewhat like a programmer configures the circuits in a computer.

Or to use another analogy, during the prime time of musical development between birth and approximately age nine or ten, the "Music

Window" is wide open. Besides your child's innate ability to hear and respond to music, a kind of "mapping" goes on in the brain whenever she has a musical experience. In that mapping, one neuron connects to another and then another, laying down tracks consisting of millions of neurons on which the "train" of musical behaviors will be able to run for the rest of her life. The more musical experiences a child has, the more "track" the child has to work with. And not only does this mapping affect musical ability, it also carries over to other skills.

"There's an overlap in the brain mechanism—in the neurons used to process music, language, mathematics, and abstract reasoning," says Dr. Mark Tramo, a neuroscientist at Harvard Medical School. "We believe a handful of neural codes is used by the brain, so exercising the brain through music strengthens other cognitive skills." It's much like saying if you exercise your body by jogging, you boost your ability not only to run but to play soccer or basketball as well, explains Tramo.[2]

During this music window of opportunity, children who grow up in families where they hear good music, are sung to by parents, get to move and sing with the music, and perhaps learn an instrument at an early age develop a much greater sensitivity to hear and respond to music—a quality we call "audiation." Dr. Edwin Gordon of Temple University defines music audiation as the ability to retain a short melody in your mind, or "hear" music that's not physically present. Through his research, Gordon discovered that music audiation develops throughout the early years and stabilizes at approximately age nine—thus the music "window."[3] Gordon also found that music audiation ability declined if the child didn't receive musical stimulation. Other researchers may disagree about the exact time the window begins to close, but this is what they all agree on: the early years are critical.

Another researcher, John Feierabend, associate professor of music education at the Hartt School of Music in Hartford, Connecticut, suggests that children deprived of music experiences in the first few years of their lives, become "music blind," unable to hear, appreciate, or enjoy the beauty that music can bring to them, just as a color-blind person isn't able to appreciate or distinguish a certain color or colors in the broad spectrum of colors that exists in the world around us. [4]

What do these studies tell us? Just as there are periods of readiness for developing reading skills or learning a foreign language, there are important periods in musical development, especially for acquiring the tools to mentally retain rhythmic and tonal patterns.

In the Music Window period, opportunities abound for growth. A California physicist, Gordon Shaw, gave weekly piano lessons to a group of three- and four-year-olds in one preschool. After six months, the preschoolers, who had scored only average on a standardized test of spatial reasoning *before* the piano lessons, scored 34 percent above average *after*. The children who were not given piano lessons showed no improvement in their scores.[5]

This study points up one of the benefits of early musical training: the positive effect on spatial reasoning needed for achievement in math and science. But music contributes much more to a child's developing brain: it enhances the child's social, cognitive, motor, affective, and creative skills, and it bolsters higher-level thinking. Music also aids in the development of visual, auditory, and language skills, develops hand-eye coordination, and improves dexterity and small muscle development.

"Music in early childhood develops lifelong abilities and sensitivities that enrich everyday life for all people. Neglect of that development in early childhood causes an irreversible loss of that potential," says Feierabend.[6] Besides all the "brain-boosting" qualities, music brings a richness to kids' and adults' experiences—a wonder, joy, and beauty that are unsurpassed.

Unlocking Musical Potential

Two important points to remember. One, although I'm going to share some basic characteristics of musical abilities for different ages in the pages that follow, remember that these don't comprise a definitive list, but offer a general framework as you plan experiences and goals for your child. Kids progress and develop at different rates. When it comes to brain development, as well as music development, each child has his own timetable, or inner clock.

Two, because musical ability is developed primarily in a relationship—especially in positive emotional interactions between parent and child—*your involvement* in any music activities is a big plus. Music teachers may be part of the picture later on, but in the early years, creating a positive musical environment at home and being involved with your child in simple music activities enhance development more than anything else. You may think that because you're not a professional musician or music teacher you can't help your child in music. Not so! People who grow up to be successful professional musicians have one factor in common: their parents sang a lot around the house. This is good news, and it's why we're going to focus on easy, "at-home" activities you can do with your child in the course of your everyday life.

Understanding what's going on musically in young children will help you to provide the best kinds of experiences to nurture your child's musical development. It'll also help you to avoid conveying inappropriate expectations or committing to lessons that are not appropriate for your child's developmental level. As your child grows, new abilities and opportunities emerge. It's like a new "chip" fires off in the brain approximately every six months. That means if your child, at age three, wasn't able to hear and sing right on pitch, he may be quite able to at age four or five if he continues to listen to and participate in music activities.

We'll look first at what we know about the natural musical abilities of children in several different stages and then explore some ways to enhance their enjoyment and aptitude and keep the Music Window open for learning.

What We Know: Babies Love Beethoven

Sensitivity to Music

What do babies know about music? Lots! They are sensitive to rhythm, intonation, and frequency variation (without ever having had any Suzuki piano lessons!). Even in the first days of life, infants can discriminate between musical styles. How do we know this? One of the many studies that showed how sensitive babies are to music involved premature infants, many of whom were critically ill and developmentally delayed. Yet the babies clearly responded to Beethoven's "Moonlight Sonata" with a lower heart rate, lower blood pressure, and lower respiratory rate than they did when they heard Khatchaturian's "Sabre Dance."[7]

Music and Mommy

Newborns recognize their own mother's voice. They can even differentiate between their mother's voice and the sounds of other women's voices.[8] Throughout childhood, starting soon after delivery, music is an important part of the emotional bonding and connection between mother and child.

Musical Memory

In addition to all these abilities, infants have good musical memory. Research shows that babies six months old and younger can learn tunes well enough to respond with delight when they hear them played.[9]

Little Mimics

Toddlers are great imitators. Toddlers learn music by repeating and mimicking what they hear. Some can even imitate voice tones and pitch. They rock, sway, move up and down to the music, and enjoy clapping and action songs.

Preschoolers' Progress

Preschool children can usually keep a regular beat, and some can sing in tune. They enjoy rhythm instruments, music, and movement for the fun and delight of making music rather than for performance or skill development.

Group Music

By the time they're in elementary school, children love music-making in a group. They can sing complete songs from memory and pick out simple tunes on musical instruments. They continue

to enjoy marching and skipping to music and have a longer attention span for cooperative music activities in a group.

What You Can Do: Music Window Openers

Wherever your child is in the range of age or skills described
above, remember that every child has some natural musical ability
(even if he can't carry a tune right now) and can benefit from musical experiences. Here are some ways to encourage your children
throughout their growing-up years with some "Music Window
Openers."

Sing songs. Singing to your baby while feeding, bathing, and
riding in the car—soft, repetitive refrains like "Rock-a-Bye Baby,"
"Twinkle, Twinkle, Little Star," "Jesus Loves the Little Children,"
lullabies and nursery songs, and of course your own favorite
melodies—is wonderful stimulation. Clap his little hands together
and move his arms and legs to the rhythm. At the same time, be
aware of how much stimulation your child can receive without
being overloaded.

Speak with baby in a singsong, rhythmical way. This is a
gentle, almost melodic conversational style sometimes called "par-
entese" or "mothertalk," where we pause between words so baby
can hear each sound. The slightly higher-pitched lyrical speech
catches baby's attention. When trying to comfort and soothe baby,
we naturally speak in a lower, slower pitch.

Tap into the Mozart effect. While at home or in the car, listen to Mozart, Beethoven, Vivaldi, and other classical music, and
you'll be tapping into the "Mozart effect," how certain types of classical music can help the brain learn more effectively. If you don't
have classical CDs or cassettes, turn on a classical radio station.

What's so important about classical music during the Music
Window years of a child's life? Georgia Governor Zell Miller is so
convinced of the benefits he made funds available so that every new-
born child in Georgia (more than 100,000 a year!) would be sent
home from the hospital with a tape or CD of classical music. Sci-

entists believe that the structured, complex melodies of classical music "warm up the brain" and enhance learning because they are similar to the complex neurological patterns of brain activity. In one study, for example, college students who listened to ten minutes of Mozart's "Sonata in D Major for Two Pianos" scored 30 percent higher on a spatial-temporal test than when they had ten minutes of silence, repetitive music, or relaxation tapes.[10] Listening to other classical composers such as Beethoven, Bach, Brahms, Schubert, and Strauss can yield similar positive results.

Since the childhood years are golden opportunities for music, give your child the best—classical music, the best jazz, folk music, instrumental music, and music from your culture and religious tradition. Hearing a Mozart piano concerto can be a wonderful way for baby to relax before nap time. Playing a lively march can put a positive spin on morning time.

Try experimenting with various types of music: play one kind while your children work on math skills for a week; then try a different era of music the next week. Was there a difference in their performance levels?

Introduce your toddler to music activities. Make music fun, not serious work. You can progress from playing "patty-cake" with your baby to "Ring Around the Rosie" and other games that connect words and melodies with gestures and movement. Remember "I'm a Little Teapot" or "Itsy Bitsy Spider"? For older kids, "Musical Chairs" or "London Bridge" are fun games. Play different rhythms, giving your child a sense of loud and soft, high and low; hand her a rhythm instrument to keep time to the music. Different instruments, like recorders, keyboards, and drums, are fascinating and fun for young children to play.

Be creative in helping your little ones make instruments. Encourage your child to strum on a cooling rack with a bowl scraper. Securely sew bells onto Velcro bands to go around little ankles and wrists. Shakers with rice in a plastic container or clackers made from two wooden spoons make interesting noises. Fill a new can (with a lid similar to a paint can) with various items and hammer it shut. Make drums out of oatmeal containers; explore sounds using kitchen utensils.

Do dance exercises at home. The desire in most kids to move and dance is natural. Ballet and tap are great, but you don't have to have lessons to enjoy movement. Turn on some music and have kids dance, skip, and hop to different rhythms. They can imitate swans, sailboats, or eagles.

Start your child in music lessons. Between ages two and a half and four, depending on your child's interest and aptitude, you could take your child to a developmentally appropriate music program specially designed for young children, like Suzuki, Yamaha, Kodaly, or Orff.

Piano and violin lessons are great, but if you can't handle the expense of lessons, get a recorder or keyboard and teach your child yourself. It's wise to wait until about age seven, when reading instruction is well under way, to tackle reading music; but the preschool music methods mentioned above are delightful group experiences designed especially for early childhood. Keep in mind that one of the main ingredients of successful music lessons is *family support*.

> **TIP:** Make sure music lessons aren't "all work and no play." A child's enjoyment is a high priority, so encourage having fun in addition to practicing.

Make a game out of pitch-matching with your preschooler. Sing "What do you want for lunch?" and suggest your child mimic the melody as she answers, "Oh, I'd like to have peanut butter!" Or play "Clap-a-Rhythm": you clap a simple rhythm pattern and your children repeat it just as they heard it.

Use music to strengthen your child's memory. If your child is learning a new skill that requires memorizing something, music helps. Do you find it easier to memorize Scripture verses when you sing them? Did you ever try to remember items on a list by reciting them to a beat? Music makes it possible to retain information by imprinting in the brain not only the words but also the elements of the music.

Let me explain. Music requires sounds performed in a measurable pattern of time. You might compare this to the ticking of a clock. A time signature results when accents are added to the notes. This accounts for the difference between a waltz and a march tune. To jazz up the latter, increase the tempo (slow vs. fast), crank up the volume (soft vs. loud), and add a dash of wild accents. Harmonize the various instruments and you have the beginnings of a great football half-time show!

Compare that to the romantic waltz you heard last summer at a wedding. It was slower, softer, and smoother than that grand old march! Chances are that you heard violins instead of trumpets. And because of those differences, you probably have a very different emotional memory of that waltz.

So what does any of this have to do with *learning?* Since the elements of music are processed and retained on the right side of the brain and language is processed on the left side, a person literally utilizes more brainpower when learning with music. There are more envelopes available to hold information when both sides of the brain are cooperating.

If you want your child to learn some new information, try setting it to music—to a rhythmic beat or familiar melody. The tune of "Good King Wenceslas" works well for helping a young child memorize his telephone number. The months of the year, multiplication tables, or the Fruits of the Spirit listed in Galatians 5:22–23 can all be learned more effectively if set to music.

For school-age children, get and stay involved with their music activities. Support daily practice. Have a music or talent night periodically as part of your family time, where each person can sing a song, do a dance, play a tune on an instrument, or even recite a poem.

If the school your child attends has music as part of the curriculum, support the music activities offered. If your child is taking piano, violin, or other lessons, find places for him to bring joy to others by sharing his music, whether it's for grandparents, senior citizens at a nearby nursing home, or a children's hospital. Sharing with and performing for others keeps kids motivated. And your personal involvement with music is a powerful booster. George, a dad I know, started guitar lessons during a time his ten-year-old son Jon was in a "slump" in his guitar lessons and wanted to quit. The two of them started practicing together and playing guitar just for fun, and Jon got reinspired. At fifteen, he's still taking lessons and improving his guitar skills.

Take your children to live performances of music. Good choices are the local symphony orchestra, string ensemble programs at nearby universities and colleges, and music festivals and events. Nothing fires up children's interest in making music and learning to play an instrument like seeing musicians performing live.

Make music part of your family lifestyle, and remember, it's never too late to begin lessons. Don't let the "window" concept limit your child's options or be an excuse. While it is true that almost all professional musicians started lessons in their childhood, many people began to play a musical instrument later in life. They may not be playing at Carnegie Hall, but they enjoy the tremendous benefits of making music. Although new research suggests that early experiences and lessons make learning to play an instrument easier, we know that if there are new challenges, the brain continues to grow throughout life.

Music Resources

Kids Make Music, Babies Make Music Too by Lynn Kleinen, and *Music for Developing Speech and Language Skills in Children, A Guide for Parents and Therapists* by Donald Michel, Ph.D., and Janet Jones, M.A. Both are available from the Music Is Elementary catalog, phone 800-888-7502, or on the Internet at www.musiciselem.com.

A Young Musician's Classical Library. Eighteen cassettes explore the music and lives of great composers. Available from Friendship House, phone 216-871-8040.

The Top 100 Masterpieces of Classical Music. Favorites from Bach, Mozart, Beethoven, Tchaikovsky, and others performed by the world's best orchestras and musicians. Great for family listening. Available from Friendship House, phone 216-871-8040.

The Classical Kids Series: Beethoven Lives Upstairs, Mozart's Magic Fantasy, Vivaldi's Ring of Mystery, and *Mr. Bach Comes to Call.* Award-winning audio and video tapes for children that combine the musicians' compositions with a riveting narrative of their lives. Distributed through Children's Bookstore Distribution, phone 416-538-7339.

Young Person's Guide to the Orchestra by Benjamin Britten. Britten has taken a theme by Thomas Tallis and given each instrument of the orchestra an opportunity to play it alone in a characteristic setting, then together with the rest of the orchestra. This guide helps children become acquainted with the different types of instruments in an orchestra. Available at music stores.

Local colleges and libraries are tremendous resources for live orchestra and provide opportunities for kids to meet the musicians after a performance. Besides city symphony events, there are also classical performances on television and on classical radio stations that you can play in the home or car.

Music Window Closers to Avoid

Don't demand technical excellence. A child has layers of concepts to incorporate when learning to play an instrument. First, hand positions, note names, and time signatures need to be mastered. Then a child learns various ways of striking keys to produce different sounds. Now add the challenge of playing both hands together. If this isn't enough to stress a new performer, add dynamics, tempo, correct rhythms, meter, and slurs. Be sensitive to your child's limits and frustration.

Let your child experiment with these advanced concepts while he's integrating them with the primary elements of instrumental performance. Nothing destroys a child's determination to excel quicker than the critical words of the person he loves the most—you!

Don't live through your child by demanding musical success. Let your child's performance be a reflection of his own desire to achieve. Sometimes parents who tried to excel in music and met with limited success push and force their offspring to live out the parent's hidden dreams of excellence in music. This trap will dampen your child's love for music. Let your child grow musically in the fertile soil of praise and patient understanding that you provide.

Be patient with your toddler's musical noise. Little ones have their own ideas of how loud a song should be "sung." They might love the intense pounding of a wooden spoon on an overturned kettle. Their rhythms might not coincide with that of the music being heard, but they are happily playing along. Rather than helping your toddler to beat in time or to play softer, step back and let him go. Perhaps this would be a good time to retreat into the kitchen and make a soothing cup of tea!

Steer away from preschool music programs and schools where the emphasis is on the "product," i.e., the performance. These programs tend to squelch creativity rather than enhance children's musical development. Music classes for preschoolers that are performance-oriented (children are taught they must sing in a certain style, and everything is focused on putting on a splashy performance in extravagant costumes) probably are more for the adults instead of the children.

If you do choose a preschool music program or class for your child, choose carefully and observe a class or two before enrolling. And remember, many of the same music-making activities these programs offer (singing, dancing, and movement) can be done at home without pressure in a nurturing and loving environment.

If your child sings off key, don't think he has no potential for music. Sometimes we feel that music lessons are only for kids who show early talent in music. Don't fall into that trap and limit your child's opportunities to make music. While some children sing in tune and stay on pitch early, others are late bloomers. For some, learning to play a musical instrument is easier due to different levels of dexterity or hand-eye coordination. Every child has some musical aptitude—the capacity to respond to musical sounds and to control the body's movement in order to create music. Avoid comparing your children if one seems to progress faster than the others. Let them each go at their own pace.

Making music isn't only for those who do it with ease or have the talent to perform professionally. Playing an instrument is a skill that can be learned, developed, and polished. And every child has great potential to enjoy and make music for a lifetime.

Heavenly Father,
Thank you for the gift of music.
You've made our hearts sing, put music in the air for us to enjoy,
given us the capacity to enjoy hearing and making melodies of our own.
Give me wisdom as a parent to choose the best music
to fill our home and enrich my child's life.
Help me see ways to help him develop his full music potential
and, most of all, to be a model of one who gives music back to you—
the Music Maker—in praise and worship.

Seven

the language window

Every child ought to know the pleasure of words so well cho-
sen that they awaken sensibility, great emotions and under-
standing of truth. This is the magic of words—a touch of the
supernatural, communication which ministers to the spirit, a
gift of God. [1]

GLADYS HUNT

As I was mixing ingredients for a cake this week, I held Caitlin, our six-month-old granddaughter, and narrated the process ("Caitlin, we're making a yummy birthday cake for your daddy!"), pointing out utensils and ingredients: "bowl," "water," "mixer," "eggs" while letting her touch the cold, smooth egg and other objects. Zing! Zip! Zap! Neurons from her ears made connections with the auditory part of her brain. A smile lit up Caitlin's face as I gave her a tiny taste of batter. Her eyes widened in attention as she touched the stainless steel mixer and felt the sugar.

Suddenly our Sheltie dog walked in and I bent down and said "Doggy" as Caitlin stretched out a hand to pet Joy's soft fur. Zap! Zap! Neurons from the sensory motor area of her brain made connections with the language area.

Caitlin can't say "Let's bake a cake" or read a recipe yet, but all the words, sights, sounds, and tastes she experienced in our cooking time and every day throughout her first months of life are forming a language map in her brain. As linguists study brain development, they are finding that kids learn language in more amazing ways than we ever thought possible. During this critical time of the "Language Window," the first few years of life, the brain is wired for a lifetime of learning, speaking, reading, writing, and creating.

Although the word "infant" means "without speech," the definition is deceiving, because even in the earliest months infants are attempting to imitate Mom and Dad and others as they speak. They're not only trying to talk, they also mimic the "turn-taking" aspect of real conversation, and by six months can already discern the sounds they'll later need for speaking. Babies are perceptive listeners who are even more interested in adult voices than in music.[2]

What We Know: Recent Discoveries

Let's take a look at some recent discoveries about the language skills of babies and young children:

A Big Vocabulary

While most kids can't tell time or tie their shoes by age three, they've already acquired a surprisingly large vocabulary of thousands of words. Their understanding of words may exceed their ability to say them by 100 to 1.[3]

How do they accomplish this linguistic feat? Language development begins long before delivery; babies get a head start while hearing Mom's voice, a bit muffled, in the womb. Language learning accelerates at birth and, at only four days old, infants can distinguish one language from another and are extremely sensitive to the sounds around them.[4]

We got to observe this sensitivity firsthand when Caitlin was in an NICU (Neonatal Intensive Care Unit) her first three weeks of life. Although sedated and hooked up to a noisy, high-powered ventilator that was breathing for her, Caitlin could hear every word and sound. When she was most critical, doctors advised us not to speak around her or even touch her because in hearing and responding she would use up precious energy that she needed just to breathe. As I am writing this section, she is a very verbal six-month-old who babbles very expressively, much to the delight of her parents and grandparents!

Within the first three months, babies start memorizing words and adding them to their verbal database without knowing their meanings. By eight to nine months, their brains begin to connect words with the definitions. And by eighteen months, they're learning new words and their meanings every day.[5]

A Big Capacity for Processing Information

Babies' brains have the potential to take in large amounts of information and find the regular patterns and associations in that information. Because of this, infants and young children have a much bigger capacity for learning language than previously thought possible.[6]

Little Grammarians

This ability may surprise you the most. Although toddlers can't diagram sentences, by age two they are learning grammar patterns just by listening and can tell what's correct and what's not. And 90 percent of the sentences spoken by the average three-year-old *are* grammatically correct![7]

Mega-Memory

By the time babies are eight or nine months old, their memories are fully functional, so be careful what you say around your tots. They remember a big percentage of what they hear!

Foreign Language Facility

Young children can learn several different languages rather effortlessly if exposed to them early in life. Patricia Kugh, a psychologist at Seattle's University of Washington who has done extensive research with babies' language development, calls infants up to four months "universal linguists" because of their ability to perceive speech sounds of all languages. That's because your child doesn't know what language she's going to be speaking (at least not at birth), so her brain is equipped to learn any language![8]

But while an infant's brain can perceive and respond to all of the 150 sounds that make up human speech, by ten months of age they've become specialists, zeroing in on the sound patterns in the language they hear at home. They have learned to filter out foreign sounds that they could produce but don't ever hear.[9]

Because the foreign language abilities "window" is from birth to about age ten, if you want your child to master a second language, introduce it by the age of ten; don't wait until high school! Age is particularly crucial in pronunciation. Studies show that kids younger than puberty have the highest probability of achieving a near-native pronunciation. After puberty, that probability drops to almost zero no matter how many years the person lives in a foreign country. (See "Encouraging foreign language learning," p. 105)

The Auditory Map

By the age of twelve months, a major part of a child's basic auditory blueprint is formed. The more words he hears by age two, the larger his vocabulary will be. By about ten months, babies begin to add gestures to words (like shaking the head with "No!" or waving when they say "Bye-bye!"). Toddlers link words to meaning and start naming things. By the fireworks display of language that occurs around eighteen months, it's obvious new words and meanings are added daily.[10] The brain circuitry that provides the foundation for a lifetime of learning, communicating, reading, and writing has been formed and will continue being wired until approximately age ten.

Baby Talk

While the first real words usually are spoken between ten and eighteen months, babies engage in cooing ("oohs" and "aahs"), then babbling ("ba-ba-ba"), and move quickly to combining different sounds. By four to seven months, first language sounds like "eee-eee" and "ooo-ooo" appear, and by seven to nine months the first well-formed syllables like "da-da" or "ma-ma"—music to your ears!—are heard.

By six months, children engage in "lalling," which is making a sound and then repeating it. By nine or ten months they begin repeating or echoing what parents are saying, and at about eleven months some children begin using words with meaning or engaging in "baby talk"[11] (which has the actual rhythm of speech but the words often don't make sense to grownups. They make perfectly good sense to the child, however). By approximately 18 months (and earlier for some children), kids start stringing words together in simple two-word combinations like "Drink juice" and "Daddy come."

What You Can Do: Language Window Openers

With this tremendous capacity for learning during the Language Window, you can see what a golden opportunity we have as parents. But keep in mind that all kids don't reach these language progress points at the same time; there can be variances of up to a year. The language environment of a child makes a big difference in what verbal skills develop. Children in a language-rich home environment, surrounded by words, are usually fluent speakers by age three. Kids who are language-deprived in their early years rarely master communication even as adults, regardless of the training they get.[12]

Your home is the best language classroom in the early years. What you do and say impacts your child's vocabulary and language ability more than anything else! See suggestions below for enriching it even more.

For example, we know that infants whose moms naturally talked a lot to them during their first year knew 131 more words at twenty months than did babies of quieter, less involved mothers. By twenty-four months, the toddlers of talkative mothers knew 295 more words! Hearing the sounds of words builds circuitry in a child's brain so it can absorb more words.[13]

Here are some ways to develop your child's language abilities at home:

Talk—Talk—Talk!

Since the more you talk to your baby the more extensive the language "mapping" in the brain will be, the best thing you can do is talk up a storm in a colorful, interesting way. From birth, get close and talk to your child lovingly and gently. Get close to baby's face and carry on a "conversation," taking turns. Speak to your baby and then give your baby an opportunity to respond.

"Oh, you're happy today? What shall we do today?" As baby shakes her rattle, you might say, "Yes, we'll play today! Let's stroll you over to the park and play."

With your baby in a stroller, talk about what you're seeing while walking through the neighborhood. Chat while you're playing with her at the park, folding clothes, bathing her. Describe ingredients when you're cooking a meal in the kitchen. Such dialogues keep your child engaged in the activity at hand and, at the same time, build a rich storehouse of vocabulary.

Narrating events and naming objects as you hold your baby are valuable language activities. Show him the birds flying by the window and the first snowflakes falling. Explain what's happening. When naming objects, use the correct names and be consistent; avoid confusing your baby by calling the cat "Kitty" today and "Mother Cat" tomorrow and "The Meow" the next day. Whenever possible, make eye contact with baby when you're talking so he can see how your lips move and he'll stay tuned in and interested.

When you're in the car together on errands, tell your child where you're going. At mealtime, comment on the food: "Here are your carrots; here are two apple slices—one, two. Here's your spoon." Point to and label objects as you move through grocery store aisles; discuss what you're seeing on the television news; label toes and nose and ears while you're changing diapers or playing. As your child grows, ask her to narrate her activities from an afternoon at Grandma's house or at a friend's.

All these conversations from everyday life are important links in your child's language learning. Lucy Calkins, mother of two sons and author of *Raising Lifelong Learners*, says, "Although I searched diligently for a nursery school that supported talk (and, therefore, thought) I have always believed that, for oral language development, Dorothy from *The Wizard of Oz* was right—'There's no place like home!'"[14]

Home is the *best place* to develop your child's language skills. You don't have to be a constant chatterbox, but remember that the more interesting and lively Mom's and Dad's conversations are, the richer your children's vocabularies are and the more extensive the circuitry for language that is built up in their brains.

Read Aloud

Your child may not be able to repeat all the words or comprehend the plot yet, but hearing the rhythms of *Goodnight Moon* or a Mother Goose poem and the sounds, repetition, and cadence of speech in *The Little Engine That Could* is important to her developing language skills. Books with rhymes and songs are especially fun for infants and young children.

Even after children can read for themselves, *reading aloud is important*. In an average American school, kids spend approximately two hours a day completing worksheets and exercises but only *twelve minutes* reading books.[15] If they don't read regularly at home, kids are unlikely to become fluent readers.

Play Games, Sing Songs with Movement and Finger Play

Repetition is the key to learning anything, and songs with movements that connect with the words are a happy way to keep young children's attention and expand their language at the same time. "Patty-cake" and "This Little Piggy," "Ride a Cock Horse to Banberry Cross" and other old-fashioned nursery games and rhymes are fun and enhance language. As your child grows, make up riddles, rhymes, and tongue twisters.

Teach Your Child to Listen for Sounds

Help your child to be alert and learn to listen to sounds both inside the home and outside. Identify sounds by saying, "Do you hear the birds singing?" "Do you hear that siren?" As soon as your child has the vocabulary to identify familiar sounds, make a game of it: "Who's making that chirping sound?" "What's making that buzzing sound?"

Provide Resources and Time for Pretend Play

Pretend play is essential to children's growth and learning and especially to language development. In pretending, kids come to realize that one thing can stand for another—a background for understanding words as symbols (reading) and numbers as symbols (math). Encouraging your child's pretend play also develops creativity and communication skills. Start by providing a box with dress-up clothes, old costume jewelry, hats of all kinds and shapes (cowboy, fireman, baseball, etc.).

Add some dolls and doll accessories, big blocks and building toys, and stuffed animals, and for the older preschooler include some office props (kids love to play "office") and travel props, some puppets (either homemade or store-bought), and a box to make a stage. On rainy days, a sheet over a card table makes a great "tent" for kids to pretend they're camping out. Encourage your child to take along a few books and a flashlight.

Give your children the gift of some play space they don't have to keep neat and perfectly picked up, along with some unscheduled time. Then watch them think up imaginative things to play. What fun they can have for very little money!

Provide Art Materials

Paper and markers, pencils, finger paints, and clay or play dough are excellent stimulators for language growth. When your child draws a picture and you ask him to tell you the story behind it, you are encouraging conversation. Then write the words of his story below the pictures. Turn it all into a "book" with a cover made from construction paper illustrated by your child. Creating such a book is a powerful language activity that helps children understand the reading-writing connection—an essential skill for learning to write.

Encouraging Foreign Language Learning

Preschoolers and young children easily gain a foundation for learning foreign languages. A second language they experience at

Reading-with-Baby Tips

I admit it—reading to a baby is a challenge. I've been reminded of this by my grandbaby Caitlin, who, for the first nine months, has been mostly interested in eating the books! So here are some tips to keep reading interesting and fun for baby:

Read books that are just fine to chew on at first! Soft plastic books that squeak are Caitlin's favorites. Babies and toddlers also love books made especially for touching, like *Pat the Bunny,* scratch-and-smell books, texture books with flaps to lift, and books with squeakers to squeak.

Read books you love and your baby will likely enjoy them too. If you're like Caitlin's mom, Tiffany, and adored Dr. Seuss books as a kid, try reading *The Cat in the Hat* or *Green Eggs and Ham.* If you love Richard Scarry or Maurice Sendak books, read those aloud. Your delight is contagious!

Add bouncing, movement, and tapping. When I read *The Little Boy With a Drum* to Caitlin and the story says "rat-a-tat-tat," I drum on the book and she giggles. As I read "Ride a Cock Horse to Banberry Cross" from a Mother Goose book, I bounce her on my knee. To add to the fun, vary the places you read and the positions—on your lap, stretched out on a play quilt on the floor, outside on the grass.

Make baby's own book of family faces. Fill a photo album or scrapbook. Put in photos of sister and brother, Grandma and Grandpa, a favorite aunt or friend, and, of course, the family pets. Then "read" this book together and watch the enjoyment.

Choose books with repetition. Babies and young children love repetition and books like *Goodnight Moon.* Read frequently, these repetitions reinforce sounds, rhythms, and connections between words.

Stock diaper bag or backpack with a few books. Read to your child wherever you go—waiting at the doctor's office or sitting in the park.

this age doesn't sound strange to them and will be picked up more quickly later. Here are some fun ways to give them exposure to a second language.

Music is a universal language. Play a cassette of Spanish, French, German, or other culture and teach your child a song in that language.

Host an international student in a home-stay program. In the many English as a Second Language (ESL) institutes at universities around the country, host families are needed for short-term students. This is a great way to let your children hear a different language on a regular basis. One family in such a program hosted Asian students. A side benefit was that their son (who was in elementary school) learned Japanese and as a teenager has gone to Japan twice. If you can't host for a month or more, having international students for a weekend or an occasional meal is a two-way blessing. The students love to practice their English with Americans and have a home-cooked meal, and your kids get to learn about a foreign country and language!

Encourage your child's school (or homeschool group) to offer a foreign language. A foreign language can be taught in preschool, kindergarten, and elementary grades. If necessary, recruit a parent or person in the community who is fluent in the language. Even ten to fifteen minutes a day of being taught by a native or a person who is fluent in the language is terrific for "wiring" the brain for other languages. Julie, now an ESL teacher at Oklahoma City University, had thirty minutes a day of a French instructional video when she was in the fourth and fifth grades, then in seventh grade took a French class. She already knew the sounds and developed a near-native pronunciation even though she had never been to France. It was that early exposure to French spoken by a native of France that made the difference. She went on to major in languages and became a teacher of international students.

Preschools or after-school programs can have foreign language days. For example, on Spanish day, a native-speaking person comes to class, sings in Spanish, and teaches the kids a song and a few words; they eat tacos and play a game.

Language Window Closers to Avoid

Being aware of the factors that hinder the language development of children is a first step to avoiding these "Window Closers." Instead of making more circuits in the brain for language, these roadblocks *diminish* potential. Instead of encouraging good speech and communication skills, they *discourage* them. In her book *Smart Kids With School Problems*, Dr. Priscilla Vail points out that these roadblocks are in fact the unrecognized cause of many learning, behavior, and attention problems. They include day care, recurrent ear infections, weary parents, and the instant gratification of television and video.[16] Let's look at how to avoid these Language Window Closers.

The problem with day care. We know that children's listening and language skills are developed through engaging in frequent one-on-one conversations with adults. While most day-care providers endeavor to offer as much physical safety and security for kids as possible, they tend to have a much larger caretaker-to-child ratio than a mom and children at home. Because of this, a child in a reasonably warm home will have *fifty to one hundred times more* individual language interactions per day than the average teacher-child interactions in day care or the classroom. Multiply that number by 280 days of child care a year and you can see why kindergarten and first grade teachers can immediately spot the kids who have been raised at home with Mom and those who've been in day care most of their young lives.[17]

Knowing this information can help you make wise choices for your child during the critical early years. When a mom is employed, you might consider starting a home business, putting your child in home day care with a small parent-child ratio, working part-time, paying an aunt or a grandma to keep your child, having her go to preschool in the morning and be in a home situation with another mom or neighbor in the afternoon, starting your own home day care, or some other alternative rather than having your child spend all day in a large facility. When it is necessary for your child to have another caregiver, it should be someone who is extremely responsive and sensitive, who's willing to cuddle, comfort, talk, and read and provide experiences for learning.

The effect of frequent ear infections and hearing difficulties. An increasing concern in day-care settings is more exposure to bacteria and viruses—causing colds and flu that often develop into ear infections. Many research studies, such as those reported in *The Journal of Learning Disabilities*, show that frequent middle-ear infections can result in hearing loss and lowered acuity, causing a child to miss certain words and frequencies of sound.[18] Children who do not hear well miss a lot of language because hearing problems impair the ability to match sounds to letters. Their difficulty with processing sounds makes it harder for them to speak and to learn to read. They often misunderstand directions and fail to experience vocabulary growth simply because of ear problems.

When your child does get an ear infection, protect the hearing by promptly seeing a physician to treat the infection. Test early for hearing difficulties. If your child is having trouble understanding when others talk, not turning his head in the direction of a sound by six months, or not talking by thirty months, he should be evaluated by a physician or an audiologist.

Too much TV. Excessive television watching in the early years has been shown to stifle children's creativity, shorten attention span, decrease language ability, and deprive kids of conversation, questions, pretend play, and physical activity. Yet many American kids have already watched 5,000 hours of TV by the end of kindergarten. The years of the Language Window are too important to spend them in a passive pastime that stunts their verbal skills! Aim for no more than thirty minutes total per day of TV, videos, and movies, and remember, *less is always better* when it comes to television. Kids learn language skills best from *live interaction with real people!* Set some limits while your child is young and *you* hold the channel changer, because this is a window of opportunity you don't want him to miss!

As Jane Healy says, "The brain is ravenous for language stimulation in early childhood but becomes increasingly resistant to change when the zero hour of puberty arrives."[19]

Playing board games of all kinds, doing puzzles, making models, working on crafts, throwing a Frisbee, flying a kite, or taking a walk together are all terrific alternatives to watching TV that build parent-child communication.

When you do watch a show, discuss it with your child. Ask cause-and-effect questions like: "What do you think will happen now?" "Why do you think (the main character) acted like that?" Talk about what's real and true, what's false or fantasy.

Can it make a difference to limit a child's TV? The experience of a mother and speech therapist from Iowa is a good example. Because of some warnings she'd heard and what she'd observed in her daughter's behavior when she watched television, this mom was advised to establish a "No TV" policy. Once or twice a week, Rachel got to watch a videotape chosen especially for family viewing after her mom had read the book to her.

After the TV blackout, Rachel's parents began to notice a *rapid increase* in Rachel's speech and language skills. She had been sixteen months old when she said her first word, and at twenty-seven months was putting only two words together. But Rachel quickly went from two-word expressions before the blackout to *retelling* the whole *Cinderella* book, singing nursery rhymes, and using *nine words and more per sentence* after the blackout. Also, with TV limited (both hers and her parents'), Rachel engaged in "amazing amounts of make-believe" and was having so much fun, she didn't seem to miss not watching TV.[20]

Weary parents. It takes energy to talk with young children and to listen to their sometimes rambling stories and many questions once they start talking. When kids come home to weary moms who are so exhausted at the end of the day that talking and listening to their child's chatter is difficult, that cuts down on language development. When a mom is perpetually tired in the evening, a child may get a meal and hugs, but be starved for communication and interaction. If this is the case, bring in some reinforcements to interact with the child—grandparents, spouse, family friends.

Fostering Good Listening and Language Skills

Whether any of the above roadblocks are an issue or not, here are some easy ways to keep the Language Window wide open and to build good listening skills:

Dinner table talk. Make dinner table conversation a priority. Set aside some time, without the distractions of TV or telephone ringing, to eat together and talk about the day—even if you're having peanut-butter sandwiches and apple slices! Lively family discussions build a child's sense of self-esteem and belonging and develop his thinking and reasoning abilities in addition to his verbal skills.

Once kids are in school, talking about what they've learned at the dinner table *doubles* their retention and understanding. Research shows that students who do the best on mental tests and on report cards are generally from homes where there's a great deal of open communication, where the kids feel safe sharing ideas and feelings. Another study found the one common factor among students who got the highest SATs (Scholastic Aptitude Test) was they regularly had dinner with their parents![21] Make dinner a positive, warm time of talking together, and you'll be fostering good listening skills.

Follow the leader. Give your children practice following directions. Even with little ones you can start with a simple request and add to it: "Please bring Mom the magazine." Next time: "Please bring Mom the magazine and close the door."

Always add some encouragement, "Thank you! You're such a big help."

Games like "Simon Says" build listening skills in a fun way. Give an instruction, "Simon says, 'Pat your head.'" If the order is given with "Simon says," the players are to do as instructed; without "Simon says," orders are to be ignored. Those players who act without "Simon says" are "out." The last one left is declared the winner and gets to be "Simon" for the next round. Simon can add multiple instructions like: "Pat your head, tickle your nose, jump up and down," depending on players' ages.

Encourage your child's writing skills. Having a "family mailbox" made from a shoe box for written messages between parents and children, helping a child write her own books, encouraging a child to write lists, getting a grandma (or another relative) to be an "e-mail pen pal"—all are activities that encourage the writer in your child. When writing is fun, something the whole family does, a child will write more naturally.

Besides reading aloud, listen to audiotapes of stories and books. This is a pleasant activity on short or long trips or for bedtime, when you're both tired or on a night when you can't read a story aloud. Discuss the stories and books your child is listening to; ask a question about what happened or what he liked best.

Be a storytelling family. Storytelling is wonderful for children's language skills. Hearing stories ignites a child's imagination, instills good listening habits and a longer attention span, expands vocabulary, and builds special memories. There's nothing nicer than hopping up on Mom's or Dad's knee for an impromptu story that starts, "Remember the time you fell down and I gave you the Band-Aid with the happy faces and stars, and then we went to get an ice-cream cone together?"

You can also tell familiar folktales from classics like "The Three Bears" or make up your own. Tell stories about when you were a child or stories from your family's history. Make up an animal story by starting with your child's favorite animal. Name the animal with an alliteration of the child's name (Robbie Dobbie the Rabbit). Make the plot about anything your child has done recently or will be doing, and make the story end at a safe, happy place.

Whenever you tell a story, you're giving your child a gift of love and time to remember. And you're building more language circuits in your child's brain while having lots of fun. As you engage in storytelling, your child will eventually want to tell her own tales. Encourage her to start with, "When I was little..." or "Once upon a time..." or "Today at school..." Kids

> **TIP:** Stories can be told at bedtime, in the car on errands or trips, or to calm your child at the doctor's office when waiting for an injection.

can use puppets, dance and movement, or drawings to illustrate their stories. Be a good listener by listening attentively and patiently and looking your child in the eye while she talks. Hear her out and your child will know you're interested in what she says and feels.

The more your child hears adult language and practices talking and listening, whether it's in dinner-table conversation, games, storytelling, everyday chats, or in playtime, the more his language skills will develop. With encouragement, your child's natural drive to communicate, discover, and understand will last a lifetime!

Great Resources for Language Development

Scour garage sales and book fairs for educational games and books to build your child's personal library.

Become a regular at your public library, stopping weekly or bimonthly to get a new load of books. You can check out books, videos, and computer software to give your child practice in language skills. Look for resources on subjects that interest your child.

Reading aloud is a big motivator to get kids "hooked on books." Some wonderful series books are *The Laura Ingalls*

Wilder Series, American Girls, The Cooper Kids Adventure Series, and, later, the *Nancy Drew* mysteries.

Provide reading props and incentives, such as a special chair to curl up in, a snack beside a book for reading time, a book bag, or a gift certificate to a local bookstore on a birthday or special occasion or even for a smashingly great report card.

Lord, what a wonderful day it was
when my child said her first words.
Thank you for the miracle of language
and all the sounds in the world around us.
During this Language Window—full of opportunity and potential
for my child to become a skillful communicator and listener—
help me seize teachable moments to talk and read together.
And since the days go so fast, help us slow down and
have fun with language!

Eight

the math and logic window

Arithmetic is where the answer is right and everything is nice
and you can look out the window and see the blue sky—
or the answer is wrong and you have to start all over
and try it again and see how it comes out this time!

CARL SANDBURG

A five-month-old baby stares intently at two dolls that dance across a stage and then disappear behind the screen. Then a third doll hops across the stage in front of the baby's view and disappears. The researcher then whisks away one doll just before the screen is taken away. Expecting to see three dolls, but seeing only two, the baby stares longer and looks surprised. The researcher, Karen Wynn, a University of Arizona psychologist, explains that this is one way she's determined that babies have a basic ability to perceive quantities and even a rudimentary ability to add and subtract. Other researchers found more than ten years ago that older babies can distinguish at just a glance the difference between one, two, three, and four balls.[1]

Babies and young children are smarter than we think—especially in math and logic! "Children are natural mathematicians," said Dr. Thomas Armstrong, as evidenced by the way young kids who haven't yet completed a primary math workbook hop on every other brick or touch every third fence post.[2]

Max, a toddler I know, held up two chubby fingers when I asked him recently how old he was. His twin, Oliver, proud of knowing this important number, chimed in, "Two!" Numbers count to kids. We all remember rhymes like "One, two, buckle my shoe; three,

113

four, shut the door" and how proud we were when our own children learned to count to ten. It all starts in the first year during the "Math and Logic Window."

During the years from birth to age nine, circuits are wired for math and logical thinking skills. Circuits for math lie in the brain's cortex, the part of the brain that controls higher mental functions, such as thinking, planning, remembering, and analyzing.[3] Right next to these math circuits are circuits for music, which is why children who have music lessons seem to develop stronger math, logic, and spatial skills.

What We Know: Developing in Math and Logic

Here are some things we know about the wonderful world of math and logic thinking that is developing in your child:

Exploring Is Better Than Flash Cards

A nature scavenger hunt or a game of hide-and-seek may help your child's math circuits develop better than drilling her on flash cards, especially during the preschool and early elementary years. The reason for this is that a child's awareness and concepts about math are linked to physical development. Kids who get to explore and manipulate objects begin to conceptualize things in a sequence, grasp spatial relationships, and more easily understand order of movement (such as if you climb up, you have to climb down; what goes in must come out). All these are crucial concepts for math.

"Real learning is a process of discovery and if we want it to happen, we must create the kind of conditions in which discoveries are made. We know what these are. They include time, leisure, freedom, and lack of pressure," said John Holt in *Learning All the Time*.[4]

Little Kids Learn Best from Direct Experience with People and Objects

Jean Piaget, a pioneer in child development, explained in his *Theory of Cognitive and Affective Development* how children construct and acquire knowledge and the changes kids undergo in their journey to mature thinking and reasoning. Piaget believed babies up to age two are in the "sensori-motor" stage of intelligence in which they don't think abstractly but instead learn primarily through play, exploration, and concrete activities. The period from two to seven Piaget called the stage of "preoperational thought," which is characterized by the development of language skills (where the child begins to know symbols such as words and pictures) and rapid conceptual development.

Ages seven to eleven Piaget described as the stage of "concrete operations," in which children still need concrete, hands-on experiences but develop the ability to apply logical, critical thinking to concrete problems. For example, they would understand magnetism better by actually experimenting and playing with different size magnets and metal objects they attract than by looking at pictures and hearing an explanation of magnetism. And from eleven to fifteen and beyond, children become more like adult thinkers. They think abstractly and apply logical reasoning to solve a variety of problems.[5]

Understanding that young children are concrete thinkers and in the early years learn math concepts best with things they can touch, handle, and move around helps us to maximize their math circuits. Hands-on and real-life activities help guide them to discover that math is not only useful in everyday life but also fun and exciting. Circuits for math and logic thinking also develop through exploring and play and from manipulating objects (like pushing blocks through slots of different sizes).

Stages of Learning

Birth to one year: From birth to one year, babies learn mainly through the five senses. Even at the young age of six to twelve months, they learn cause and effect through dunking bath toys and playing with a jack-in-the-box. Preschoolers love to count, sort, and classify with big plastic beads, pegboards, and games. They don't need worksheets to fill their days. They don't need to sit quietly doing seatwork or memorizing addition tables. They need to be physically active. They don't need to be pushed or pressured to master skills because they are eager learners who try to discover everything in their surroundings, much like a scientist investigating a complex problem.

Early math skills like sorting and cause-and-effect thinking begin to emerge between the ages of three to eight months. When our grandbaby Caitlin waves her new rattle and it makes a noise, or she drops it over and over just to watch me pick it up, she's discovering something about cause and effect. She may not realize the consequences of things—such as if we get tired of picking up the rattle, it will likely be put away. But she's learning by trial and error. When your seven-month-old sorts blocks by size, he's practicing an important math skill. By age three, he can sort toys by both shapes and colors.

Two- to three-year-olds: Children who are two and three years old may understand number concepts such as one cat and two cats, and have a rudimentary understanding of classification, such as a dog is an "animal."[6]

Kindergarten: By kindergarten, kids have many math ideas under their thinking caps. They can understand largest and smallest, longer and shorter, closest and farthest. They can count objects as they touch them and even count to ten.

Children learn the concept of number if they are given things to play with, handle, sort, and count. They learn to count naturally with blocks, pebbles, poker chips, and buttons (of course, we have to watch the size of objects we give to a child to prevent choking). The type of object isn't important—cardboard cutouts of farm animals work as well as more expensive "counting bears" or dinosaurs.

Girls can learn numerical skills just as well as boys if they are given opportunities like those suggested below. However, parents and teachers usually don't expect girls to do as well in math as they expect boys to do. But with the encouragement of parents and teachers, all children can become good mathematical thinkers and top math achievers.

What You Can Do: Making the Most of the Math and Logic Window

Do you remember childhood games of hide-and-seek (. . .96, 97, 98, 99, 100—Here I come, ready or not!), counting during jump rope, playing hopscotch on the sidewalk? Or the enjoyment your child derived from songs and nursery rhymes that involved counting, such as "Diddle Diddle Dumpling" ("Diddle diddle dumpling, my son John, went to bed with his breeches on, one stocking off, and one stocking on. . .") or "Two Birds" ("There were two birds sitting on a stone, Fa, la, la, la, la, de; One flew away, and then there was one. . . ."). Child's play is learning!

Mathematical thinking and logical thinking consist of not only numerical skills but visual-spatial and problem-solving skills, which we'll explore later in this chapter. Yet with the innate understanding of numbers and the desire young children have to search for order and patterns in their world, there's much you can do to maximize learning during the Math and Logic Window years.

When kids get to learn from activities in which they use math for real-life purposes like those below, math becomes more fun, more like a puzzle than a chore. Here are some ways to aid the math circuitry forming in your child's brain and build a solid foundation for young children, ages two to eight:

Sorting

Let your child sort laundry into piles: Dad's dirty (or clean) clothes, Mom's, brother's, and sister's; then sort by color. Sort and categorize silverware by putting away knives, forks, and spoons in their proper slots. Sort coins into stacks of quarters, dimes, nickels, and pennies. When you do these household activities with your child, talk about what you're doing. Involve them whenever you can.

Setting the Table

Learning a pattern is foundational to math, and setting the table is a good way to practice patterns. You might ask, "Let's count how many of our family will be here tonight for dinner." Then count out what silverware will be needed. Make a placemat out of bright construction paper, and with markers indicate where the plate, glass, fork, knife, and spoon go so your child can have that model to set the table.

Someone's in the Kitchen with Mom

When you follow recipes and cook with your child, he learns about measuring, dividing portions, timing, and many other math concepts. Most kids love to help in the kitchen, so take advantage of their interest to let them learn about measuring ("These cookies take 1 cup of sugar, 2 cups of flour...."), using measuring spoons and cups. They can also learn about time ("Our muffins will be ready in 30 minutes. Tell me when the timer goes off so they don't burn."). Even babies love to stack plastic food containers, bang lids with a wooden spoon, and "pretend" to mix things up in a pot.

Your child can learn about order and sequence of events when you say, "Here's what we'll do to make French toast: first we beat the eggs, second we add a pinch of salt and vanilla." He can learn about dividing portions, which demonstrates fractions. "Here's a half banana for you and a half for me." Slice an apple into halves, then quarters before you and your child eat it. Cut sandwiches in different shapes and portions. Let your child play with, count, and nibble on Cheerios as you prepare breakfast, although the "nibbling on" may be his favorite part.

Comparing Sizes and Amounts

Asking questions like "Which apple is bigger?" or "How many grapes do you have on your plate?—one, two, three, four" or "How many oranges will it take to make a pound?" give children an opportunity to compare and think mathematically.

Counting Toys, Treats, and Other Objects

During playtime, count large plastic beads and nesting cups as your child stacks or connects them. When you help your child put toys away on shelves or in colorful bins in the playroom, count the toys. Make up a melody as you count buttons when you bundle him up in his coat. Count out raisins, M&Ms, or cookies when you serve them: "Here are your two cookies—1, 2."

When you're outside together, you can ask, "How many squirrels do you see playing in our tree?" Or, if the two of you are waiting in a doctor's office, you might ask, "How many red things are in the room?"

Puzzles, Shapes, and Blocks

Puzzles give practice in identifying shapes and matching colors. Kids learn math concepts like weight, size, spatial relationships, order, and proportion while playing with blocks. Talk about shapes you see in the world around you—rectangle buildings (some towns even have triangle buildings), a sign in a circle.

Singing Number Songs with Finger Play

Number songs that include finger play appeal to preschoolers, who love music and movement. Try "Five Frogs Sitting on a Log," "Ten Little Indians," "Five Little Pumpkins," or "Ten Bears in Bed." Encourage movement as you let your child jump, clap, or hop while you count.

Grocery Store Magic

Let your child learn about weights and measures at the grocery store. Let her weigh a pound of bananas or apples, a pound of potatoes or grapes.

When older, your child can help cut coupons to save money, help you find the items in the grocery store, and figure out the savings.

Pretend Play

Your child can play restaurant or store using real or pretend money. Play space travel using a one-gallon ice cream container for rocket fuel.

Playing Games

Games such as bean bag toss, dominoes, marbles, and bowling (when he's old enough to bowl) offer a variety of lessons. The game of bingo gives practice in number recognition. Games with dice and board games like Chutes and Ladders (our children's favorite when they were preschoolers), Candyland, Battleship, Monopoly, and Clue are terrific for developing math connections. Checkers, Connect-Four, and chess develop spatial thinking and strategic thinking.

Keep in mind that children are five or six before they begin to develop strategies to play a game, and around the age of six before they begin to understand the concept of rules. Preschoolers don't necessarily understand the purpose of rules and may enjoy free play or making up their own rules.

Card games are excellent for building math circuits. In fact, Dr. Margie Golick, a child psychologist who has worked with children with learning disabilities in Montreal, Canada, calls an inexpensive deck of cards the best educational tool available to teach a child essential math concepts of sorting and grouping; space, time, and number; and logic and problem solving.

Just the one game of Hearts, for example, provides practice in counting, categorizing, judging quantitative rank of number, maintaining a variable set, adding (including adding negative numbers), reasoning, memory, calculating probabilities, and developing strategies, all essential to mathematical thinking—and all that for a fun time together playing cards with your family![7]

Play "Concentration" to improve memory and to learn number associations and other math skills. Place a deck of cards face down on a table in straight rows. Each player takes a turn turning over two cards. If the cards match, the player gets to keep them, stacking the pairs to count at the end of the game, and gets another turn. If the cards don't make a match, he turns them face down and the next player gets a turn. Players try to remember where cards are located to make the most pairs and win the most cards.

Measuring Height and Width

Children always enjoy knowing personal numbers, like how tall they are or how much they weigh. So teach measurement by tracking your child's growth. Keep a board or door as your family measuring station, and with colored tape, record your child's height and the height of other members of the family. Ask "Who is tallest, Mom, Dad, or big sister?" With a measuring tape, measure the width of your child's bedroom or the driveway. Figure out how wide each is in feet. Small building and craft projects also offer opportunities to measure things.

Learning About Categories

How are things alike and how are they different? How can you group objects in different ways? Classifying and arranging things in order is foundational to logical and mathematical thinking; it means recognizing differences and comparing similarities of objects. Group the leaves or rocks you found on a nature walk according to color the first time, then group them according to size. When you're at the zoo, compare three animals—How are they alike? How are they different? Arrange toy cars from smallest to largest. Encourage your children to start a collection of some kind (rocks, stamps, even Beanie Babies) and keep track of how many they have.

Understanding Conservation of Numbers

Conservation of numbers (or mass) is an important math concept that young children don't fully understand until approximately age seven. Preschoolers decide how many or how much based entirely on how things look to them. For example, they are sure there is more milk when it's in a narrow 8-ounce glass than when it's poured into a wide 8-ounce glass. They're certain there are more coins when ten dimes are spread apart than when they are moved closer together.

Kids need lots of practice to grasp the concept of conservation of numbers, the idea that even though the arrangement of the coins or the appearance of the liquid in the glass has changed, the number of coins or the amount of liquid has not changed. The number, or amount, remains constant. Take eight buttons or beans. Have your child count the objects. Then put them in a circle, a triangle, and then in one straight line. Ask your child which shape has the most objects, and let him count the objects to figure out the answer. Give your child the objects and let her rearrange them. Take a handful of clay and make it into a ball and then into a long snake. Ask your child which shape has more clay.

Telling Time

Babies and toddlers have little concept of time. They want their bottle or whatever they need from Mom or Dad "Right now!" Toddler-Twos understand "in a minute," "today," and "pretty soon." But although they have an idea of what *today, tomorrow, this afternoon* mean, an understanding of *yesterday* isn't within their understanding, suggests Theresa Caplan in *The Early Childhood Years: the Two to Six Year Old*.[8] Four- and five-year-olds' sense of time develops as they understand words like *days, months, bedtime*.[9]

With at least one good-sized clock (not digital) visible in your home and an egg timer, you can point out the time during the day. You might ask, "How much time do you have to play before you go to bed?" Kids are always interested in that question! Share with your toddler, "At three o'clock we'll lie down for a nap, and at four o'clock we'll go to the park." Warnings such as "In ten minutes we'll leave for soccer" are helpful for kids to predict time.

An egg timer is fun to play with and "time" activities. How long will it take us to make cookies (or feed the dog)? How long will it take to brush your teeth? Once he can tell time, explain to your child how long the cake takes to bake; then ask him to figure out on the clock what time he'll get to help you ice and eat it.

Making a Calendar

Each month, make a calendar and let your child decorate it. Advent calendars are fun ways to count off the days until the arrival of Christmas. You can ask, "How many days until your birthday? Let's count them." Put happy faces on the calendar blocks to count down the days until a special family outing or to point out the day each week you take your child to the library for storytime and a puppet show.

Building with Blocks

Building with LEGOs and other fit-together interlocking building toys gives kids an opportunity to see how things function in space, how objects fit together to form different types of structures.

Getting from Place to Place

When you take a walk to the ice-cream store or to a friend's house, count the blocks you stroll to get there. Ask, "How long do you think it would take us to walk to our friends' house to play?" "How about to drive?" Encourage your child to predict or guess and then do it, comparing the times. If you drive, show your child how to read a map. Ask older kids things like, "How much gas will we need to fill the tank to get to the soccer field? Let's guess and then see at the service station" or "What's the speed limit?" They can help figure how long it would take to drive instead of fly to their grandparents' farm in Texas.

Computer Games, Calculators, and Sports

As your child grows and perhaps is interested in local or national basketball, football, soccer, or other team sports, he can follow games won versus games lost or the batting averages of players. Calculators are handy tools and computer programs offer lots of math games that build skills.

A Way of Thinking

Keep in mind that math is much more than just computing numbers. It's a way of thinking that involves patterns and relationships, visual and spatial skills, and strategies for organizing and analyzing information. Math involves terms and symbols, and it's something we all use in everyday life to function and solve problems. That's why any of the above activities and household chores that involve counting, organizing, sorting, categorizing, strategizing (as in card games), or measuring are all helpful for developing your child's math circuits—especially when language is included in the activity and you talk and explain what you're doing while you and your child are cooking, sorting, or playing games.

When you let your child plan how to spend her two-dollar allowance for the week, arrange the toy shelves, count rocks, sort laundry, use numbers in play or in fixing things—the circuitry for mathematical and logical thought is increased and you're providing a foundation that helps your child say, "I can!" to math challenges she'll encounter later in the classroom and in life.

Math and Logic Window Closers to Avoid

Keep counting, math games, and activities fun and not overly serious. Children respond best when activities are varied and spontaneous, taking advantage of teachable moments. Parents seem to enjoy the learning too.

Don't exert pressure to get the right answer the first time or every time, or show big disappointment over small failures. Little scientists learn by trial and error!

Don't provide *all* the answers when your child asks questions. Pose questions back to him; help him wonder, predict, and analyze. If he puts crayons back in the 48-crayon box and they don't fit, let him try a different approach to figure it out instead of taking over and saying, "I can do this faster (or better) than you." If we solve all our children's problems and make things too easy for them, they won't have the motivation to use problem-solving skills or to think for themselves.

Don't feel like you have to buy every expensive educational toy or fancy-packaged "math skill-building curriculum" on the market to build math and logic skills. Instead, use the raw materials of learning all around you. Expose your child to math in real life. Ordinary household objects, the backyard, the kitchen, the environment of neighborhood, a park, and family excursions are all great places to learn.

Avoid the pitfalls of perfection. Perfectionists won't try anything new because they hate making mistakes. Help your child approach new experiences with an understanding that mistakes are a natural part of the process of learning and of life. Focus on the learning instead of just the results or the grade.

Avoid doing everything for your child or she will miss opportunities for problem-solving and exercising her critical-thinking skills. Kids can match socks by color and brand, be allowed to arrange their own collections and items on a shelf, and dress themselves as early as possible, instead of being dependent on Mom to do everything.

Avoid saying, "I never had a mind for math" or "You'll never get that concept—you're just not good in math" when your child gets stuck with a math problem. Instead, cultivate a positive, can-do attitude by showing him all the math you use in everyday life and pointing out math in sports, cooking, home, and at work. When stuck on a difficult arithmetic lesson, make it concrete by using a pie to show fractions or beans to count and add or subtract.

Picture Books That Reinforce Counting and Math Concepts

Arthur's Funny Money by L. Hoban (New York: Harper & Row, 1981).

Caps for Sale by E. Slobodkina (New York: Harper & Row, 1970).

The Tenth Good Thing About Barney by Judith Viorst (New York: Atheneum, 1971).

Three Little Pigs retold by Janet Campbell (New York: Disney Press, 1993).

It's About Time by Dina Anastasio (New York: Grosset & Dunlap, 1993).

Telling Time With Big Mama Cat by Dan Harper (New York: Harcourt Brace, 1998).

Ten Terrible Dinosaurs by Paul Strickland (New York: Dutton, 1999).

One Moose, Twenty Mice by Clare Beaton (New York: Barefoot Books, 1999).

How Much Is a Million? by David M. Schwartz (New York: Morrow, 1993).

What We Know: Visual-Spatial Thinking

One night I walked in the room of our son Chris, then ten years old, to say goodnight. The lights were out, but there he lay in his bed, looking happy and *busy*, but with nothing to do (at least that's how it looked to me). "Chris, what are you doing?" I asked.

"When I can't sleep," he said, "I work the longest, hardest math problems I can in my mind, write the signs and draw the lines, and figure them out. Then I can relax." Although this didn't sound relaxing to me, to Chris it was better than counting sheep.

What Chris was describing was visual-spatial thinking, and it's one of the best predictors of math ability. In fact, this kind of thinking is intricately woven with math and logic skills. Dr. Jane Healy defines spatial thinking as how well kids relate their own bodies to objects outside themselves, such as how well they can find their way through a maze. Students with a poor grasp of spatial relationships, she notes, have trouble with all kinds of math tasks: fractions, estimating, geometry, and chart or graph reading.[10] That sounds pretty important! But how can we help our kids develop this kind of thinking?

What You Can Do: Stimulating Visual-Spatial Skills

Involve Your Child in Music

New studies have shown that music affects spatial reasoning (the ability to see objects in our mind's eye and how they're related, or the ability to "see" a disassembled picture of a rabbit and mentally piece it back together)[11] and that the spatial-temporal reasoning in three- and four-year-olds was impacted by weekly piano lessons. (See chapter 6, "The Music Window.") The researcher, physicist Gordon Shaw, explains this effect by suggesting that when kids play the piano, they are seeing how patterns work in space and time. Not only are their music circuits being strengthened but their spatial-reasoning circuits are also increasing.

Music activities—taking piano lessons, learning to play a simple recorder, listening to classical music, singing—will have a positive effect on the skills needed to comprehend and master math.

Make Available Large Muscle Exercise Equipment

Large muscle exercise equipment such as playground equipment for climbing helps to develop visual and spatial reasoning skills. Other good choices are balance beams (which you can make yourself with a sturdy board and cement blocks), balls of all sizes, large blocks and building toys, a sandbox, art supplies, and clay. Puzzles, which stimulate small muscle development, also stimulate spatial thinking.

Provide Opportunities to Explore and Discover

When kids climb, crawl through things, take things apart, play running games, and explore new paths, they are increasing their "conceptual mapping skills and firming up notions of direction and relationships in space and distance by physical means."[12] They can improve these skills only with active physical involvement. They can't develop the visual-spatial or conceptual skills they need by quietly sitting in a chair in a classroom.

> **TIP:** Helping your child to do simple science experiments and draw deductions from the results of the experiments strengthens your child's thinking skills.

Try a Memory Tray

To improve visual-spatial skills, get a tray out. While your child is watching, place five objects on the tray, one at a time, such as a comb, dollar bill, spoon, toy car, and pencil. Have your child look at them closely for forty-five seconds or more. Then take the tray away and have your child close her eyes and "see" the objects in her mind's eye and name them. Can she name the objects in the order placed on the tray? Or name them in reverse order? Then take one or two objects away and add new ones, repeating the game.

See and Describe

Have your child look at an interesting picture, an object such as a vase of flowers, or a new toy you place on the table in front of her. Then have her close her eyes and describe the object as vividly as possible. Next have her open her eyes and see how well she described the object.

Develop Visual Discrimination Skills

The same board games and card games mentioned in the early part of this chapter also develop visual discrimination skills (the ability to recognize objects and tell the difference between similar visual images, and the ability to see, interpret, and remember printed symbols like letters, words, and numbers).

Storytelling the Visual Way

Have your child choose a familiar story in a book and read it however many times is necessary for him to be able to tell the story orally the way real storytellers do. Suggest he picture the story by scenes in his mind—that is, create a "mental movie" of the characters doing the action, scene by scene. Then have him tell the story, adding his own gestures, dialogue, and even props. This enhances spatial skills as well as language skills.

When children have opportunities to develop math and visual-spatial thinking—visiting a hands-on science museum, planting their own small garden—their thinking skills will take off and blossom.

Open my eyes, Lord, to see all the opportunities
to help my child develop in math and logical thinking.
You've said for me to call to you and
you would tell me great and mighty things
that I do not know (Jeremiah 33:3),
and I'm calling on you now for your help
to take advantage of this marvelous Math and Logic Window of
    opportunity—
especially if this is not my forte.

Nine

the spiritual window

Give me the children until they are seven,
And anyone may have them afterward.

ST. FRANCIS XAVIER

Decorations squirted out the top of four-year-old Zack's "Helmet of Salvation" like the plume on a Roman soldier's helmet. Zack and his sister Katie were studying Paul's instructions in Ephesians 6 on putting on all of God's armor. Their mom had helped them cut up huge boxes, fit and glue the pieces together, and paint them with bright colors to create their own "armor." They identified the various parts as the "Sword of the Spirit," "Shield of Faith," and the "Helmet of Salvation." They learned what these and the other pieces of spiritual armor represent.

"We need to know the Bible to combat the enemy's darts," their mom explained as they painted. "The Helmet of Salvation means accepting Jesus as your Savior. Having the assurance that you belong to him protects your mind." The helmets were the children's favorite part of the "armor suits" and Zack wore his long after they moved on to another topic in their homeschool studies.

One night at bedtime prayers, Zack told his mom he wanted to be a real warrior with Jesus as his commander. He wanted to invite the Lord into his heart. Through that one lesson, Zack heard Christ knocking and opened the door to his Savior.

Corrie ten Boom experienced something similar through a simple play activity and began her relationship with God at a young age. Corrie had heard her parents read stories about Jesus her whole life, so he was like a member of the Ten Boom family. To her it was just as easy to talk to Jesus as it was to carry on a conversation with her father, aunts, or siblings.

One day Mrs. Ten Boom was watching little Corrie play house. Corrie knocked on a make-believe door, pretending to call on a neighbor. She knocked again and waited, but no one answered. Her mother patiently watched her play and finally said, "Corrie, I know Someone who is standing at your door and knocking right now."

Corrie describes this important moment. "Was she playing a game with me? I know now that there was a preparation within my childish heart for that moment. The Holy Spirit makes us ready for acceptance of Jesus Christ, of turning our life over to Him."

Her mother explained, "Jesus said that He is standing at the door, and if you invite Him in, He will come into your heart. Would you like to invite Jesus in?"

"Yes, Mama, I want Jesus in my heart," young Corrie answered. Then her mother took her hand and they prayed together. "It was so simple, and yet Jesus Christ says that we all must come as children, no matter what our age, social standing, or intellectual background."[1]

Making the most of the wonderful openness young children have to God during this "Spiritual Window," Corrie's and Zack's parents were wise enough to gently guide them to the Lord. Were they too young to enter into a relationship with Christ? Did their commitment "stick" and make a difference in their lives? In Corrie's case, from that point on Jesus was more of a reality to her and she began interceding for others, especially the poor people of the Smedestraat, a rough area near their street. As a young child, she wept and prayed for them whenever she passed the street, asking God to save them. Years later Corrie met eighteen girls who'd lived on that street, and all had become Christians. In Zack's case, after he asked Jesus to be Lord of his young life, he led his sister to Christ and began earnestly praying for his friends and family.

Full of Spiritual Potential

While some of the conventionally taught stages of learning we've discussed (like Piaget's labels of "sensori-motor" to describe infancy and "preoperational" to describe the preschool stage) and theories of child development can be helpful to understand how children think, learn, and process their view of the world, these stages aren't the final word on spiritual development.

In fact, just as kids have more capacity to learn music and language than we had thought, they also have much more spiritual capacity than we've understood. We often underestimate their ability to respond to God. Kids are spiritual beings, just like grownups, and there's no junior version of the Holy Spirit. They can experience God's presence in ways that leave indelible impressions. They pray powerful prayers with simplicity, faith, and compassion—and often see wonderful results!

Recently I took a group of children ages five to thirteen on a prayer walk at our Oklahoma state capitol. The children prayed with insight for our governor, for their representatives in Congress, and for the people of our state.

"Lord, give Governor Keating right thinking," prayed Grant, 9.

"Bless his family and draw them closer to Jesus," petitioned Susan.

"Help the senators make good decisions," prayed Andrew.

The kids filled the capitol with their prayers and God's love. We didn't know the specific answers that day, but we know God can do great things through people who pray, no matter their size or age.

Sometimes it's the child who leads the adult to God. A child in a Christian preschool was on the way to school with her mom when they passed an auto accident. The child immediately prayed aloud that God would protect the victims from permanent injury and give the doctors wisdom and help. Hearing this earnest yet simple prayer, the mom realized a need in her own life, talked that day with her child's teacher, and became a believer. Long ago Jesus knew children's amazing spiritual potential and pointed it out in verses like these:

"Haven't you ever read the Scriptures? For they say, 'You have taught children and infants to give you praise'" (Matthew 21:16 NLT).

"Jesus called a small child over to him and put the child among them. Then he said, 'I assure you, unless you turn from your sins and become as little children, you will never get into the Kingdom of Heaven. Therefore, anyone who becomes as humble as this little child is the greatest in the Kingdom of Heaven. And anyone who welcomes a little child like this on my behalf is welcoming me'" (Matthew 18:2–5 NLT).

"Let the little children come to me! Never send them away!" (Luke 18:16 TLB).

The challenge to spiritually parent your child during this window of opportunity is an awesome privilege and responsibility— one for which we desperately need God's help and wisdom. As Karen Henley says, "The preschool years are perhaps the most important years of a person's life. Although major changes can and do happen later, by age six or seven basic foundations have been laid within the child that will underlie the rest of his life."[2]

What We Know About Kids' Spiritual Window

While it's never too early or too late to begin spiritually parenting your child, the early years are a prime time. In the first six years you have more influence on your child than anyone else. For a short season, you are the center of your child's world. That's why we don't want to abdicate to others the nurturing and development that can take place at home, thinking it's the Sunday school teacher's job or the pastor's job to develop our kids' faith. Parents need to fully embrace the responsibility (and then share or delegate part of that responsibility at times to others). Here are some distinctive features of the Spiritual Window:

The Foundations of Faith

Studies show that most people who receive Christ do so between the ages of four and fourteen,[3] so your child's early years are the golden opportunity for faith to root and grow. Another survey revealed that 80 percent of missionaries received their call to the mission field when they were children—not when they graduated from college or seminary![4] When those missionaries experienced God's guidance, even though they were very young, it impacted their life decisions.

The most important spiritual qualities are developed during infancy, says Sybil Waldrop. "Trust is born of dependency on the part of the baby whose needs are supplied upon demand with tender care by the one upon whom the child depends. Thus dependency and compassion combine to *give birth to trust.*"[5]

The Role of Parents

Parents build the environment for their children to learn to know, hear, and listen to God. When you point out God's goodness in the wonder of a summer rain or sunrise, when you kneel by your child's bed to talk to God, when you thank him for food and sunshine, when you read the Bible and have family devotions—although your child may not understand everything you're saying, you are laying the foundation for the child's relationship with God.

Teaching children about God as you go along in your day is a biblical way of building spiritual foundations. Deuteronomy 6 advises parents to commit themselves wholeheartedly to loving God with all their heart, soul, and strength; to obeying his commands; and especially to teaching God's ways to their offspring. "Repeat them again and again to your children. Talk about them when you are at home and when you are away on a journey, when you are lying down and when you are getting up again" (6:7 NLT). That sounds like a lifestyle kind of Christianity, passing on the baton of faith by not only modeling your devotion to God but also instructing your children in how to love and obey God. This imparting of God's commands and ways is to take place when we're driving, eating, sitting down—anytime we're with our children—and implies that we're going to spend much of our time together.

Since young children tend to learn best in concrete, hands-on ways, we can use prayer games, storytelling, art, and other creative activities to impart spiritual truths to them. Some examples are: using a plastic globe-ball of the world to pitch around to each person in the family, letting each person take a turn to put their hand on a country and pray for its people, and drawing what they want to express to God; making the "armor" described in Ephesians 6 as Zack did; pointing out God's handiwork and sharing an object lesson through it; using an illustrated prayer journal where your child puts photos of people God has put on her heart to pray for and later draws pictures to show the answers.

Memorizing Scripture

The Spiritual Window years are opportune times to memorize Scripture. Paul described Timothy as a young man who, from infancy, knew the Scriptures (2 Timothy 3:15). And just as kids are smarter than we think, just like Timothy, they can store up more Scripture than you may think.

In Awana, a children's program that's in thousands of churches around the country, three-year-olds learn 22 verses their first year. Four-year-olds memorize 36 verses, and first graders learn a total of 56 verses. Second graders learn 77 verses; third graders, 80; fourth graders, 105 verses. Every year after that, students learn more than a hundred verses. A child who stays in the program from preschool through high school memorizes a total of at least *763 verses* from the Bible!

How Kids See God

The loving relationship between children and parents lays the foundation for children's primary attitudes toward God, their heavenly Father. Perhaps sometimes we wish this were not so because it puts a lot of responsibility on us, but kids tend to see God through the filter of Mom and Dad. The experience of my friend Jennifer Rothschild with her son's first name for his mom underscores this principle.

When Clayton was nine months old, he added "Da-da" to his first distinguishable word "ball." Whenever he wanted something from Dad, he prefaced it with "Da-da!" His parents were thrilled by his first brilliant words, but after a few months Jennifer grew sad that he hadn't called her "Ma-ma" yet. She thought the baby didn't call her anything.

Then one day, listening a little closer to what Clayton was saying, she realized he was referring to her as "God." When he wanted juice, he said, "God, juice!" This was amusing at home, but in public when she told Clayton it was time to go and he wailed, "God! God!" or he called out "God! Juice!" it became embarrassing.

"Don't worry," the pediatrician said when this young mother expressed her concerns. "Sometimes kids pick their own names to call parents or grandparents." But *God? How did he come up with that?*

One day as Jennifer was preparing dinner, with her baby playing beside her, she understood. He saw her fix the food and then, moments later, they sat down, bowed their heads, and said, "Dear God, thank you for this food!" Because his mom had made the food, Clayton had decided she must be God. Much to her relief, when Clayton was about fourteen months old, he finally started calling her "Ma-ma."

Though a humorous incident the family can now look back on and chuckle about, what a picture this was to these young parents of how we are our kids' first picture of their spiritual Father. Parents are God's representatives, and everything we say and do reflects him. We're temporarily at the center of our kids' world and our love reflects God's love, a love so intense he gave his own Son for our salvation—a loving God who cares enough to provide for our needs, comfort us when we hurt, and never leave or forsake us. This thought would bring even the most confident parent to his or her knees!

Developing Faith

The most helpful way I've found of looking at a child's spiritual journey comes from Art Murphy, a minister for children in Florida:

Discovery Stage

The first is the Discovery Stage, which extends from birth to seven years of age. In this time of sowing faith-seeds in our children's lives, they soak up everything, especially through the five senses. This is a great make-believe time as preschoolers often operate in what's called "magical thinking." When you explain the Trinity, they may be thinking of the Easter Bunny, Santa, and the Tooth Fairy rather than the Father, Son, and Holy Spirit (or, as someone suggested, they may picture God as someone who watches over everyone and gives away toys and pets).

But kids are energetically seeking to discover everything they can about the world around them. Young children are constantly finding out new information. They soak up all that they see and experience: the behavior of parents, siblings, and friends; Bible stories read to them; TV programs. Little by little faith emerges in the Discovery phase. Sometimes it's mixed with misinformation. A three-year-old I know recited John 3:16 like this: "For God so loved the world, that He gave his only *forgotten* son . . ." and his friend next to him finished it with: "that whosoever believe in him should not perish, but live *happily ever after.*"

Though your young child may not understand all the spiritual words he hears at home or in Sunday school—or even all the verses he memorizes in family devotions and vacation Bible school—he's recording this information in memory much like a tape recorder collects sounds, and he may surprise you later by parroting them.

One day a mom who was ill was lying on the couch, trying to keep an eye on her three-year-old son. He tried to use his doctor kit to fix up his mom, then, tired of that, he said it was time for him to preach. While his feverish mother lay with her eyes closed, the preschooler set her lap desk on the coffee table as a "podium." Standing at the podium, he dramatically pounded his fist on the table and shouted, "Death comes unexpectedly!" a line straight out of the movie "Pollyanna." His mother sat straight up, startled not only at her son's message but also at his sharp memory!

With curiosity at its height in the pre-K years, the more verbally expressive children will ask many questions about what they're learning, while the quieter ones may not verbalize any ideas. But they are all thinking, observing, and discovering. Praying for your child throughout spiritual labor and delivery as well as all the stages of spiritual, mental, and emotional development is just as important as praying for your child from conception to physical delivery at birth.

The Discerning Stage

The Discerning Stage begins in the early elementary grades but can occur as early as age four or five. Every child is unique and on his own timetable and, most important, on God's timetable, but there are some patterns emerging.

In this second stage of faith, kids ask more specific questions: "What happened when Grandma died?" "Where is heaven? Can I go there?" They are testing ideas. They start to wonder how the Bible stories and spiritual concepts they hear from parents and Sunday school teachers apply to them. They may express confusion—"I want to ask Jesus into my stomach"—or take you literally, like the five-year-old boy who picked up a knife after church and said, "Mom, how do you become a Christian? How do you open up your heart? Does it hurt?" Listening to your child's questions is important.

Sometimes parents think insightful questions mean that the child is ready to make a serious commitment to Christ and may ask the minister to baptize the child. Murphy tells the eager parent, "Life is coming, but it may not be delivery time yet!"

What's most important in the Discerning Stage is for parents and other caring adults to model a vibrant, joyful faith as they aid children in learning about Jesus—reading Bible stories, memorizing Scripture—and discern God's timing. "We're the pediatricians but God is the obstetrician. He has their spiritual birth planned just as he did their physical birth," says Murphy. Some children understand the invitation at the end of a service and can have a genuine experience with Christ that leads to commitment; others are not ready at this stage. By talking, listening, asking questions, and praying with your child, you will understand your child's spiritual awareness and development.

The Deciding Stage

The Deciding Stage draws a line between kids' curiosity and real conviction. This is when the child has decided he or she wants to make a commitment to Christ.

"Don't push them or turn them away; hold out your hand as if saying, 'I'm going to lead you in God's direction,'" Murphy advises.

I remember when our son Chris made that decision. As a nine-year-old he was quiet and reflective; he'd been dedicated to God as a baby and attended church all his life. One Sunday he said to his dad and me, "I've decided I want to be baptized. I want to follow Jesus. I've already asked him to be my Lord. When can I be baptized?" Was it the death of his grandma the year before and the conversations we had about heaven? Was it the Scripture that had been stored up in his mind and heart since preschool years? Maybe he realized he needed the Lord. Whatever the combination, it was God's "right time" for Chris. After some questions and conversations, his commitment was sealed several weeks later as he was baptized—and what a memorable day it was!

As Karen Henley says, children in this stage are starting to sense their own need for God, and perhaps that's why so many between the ages of seven and thirteen make a commitment to Christ. "In the years before, Mom and Dad could solve any problem. But now children begin to see that there are problems even Mom and Dad can't solve. All of this adds up to a strong sense of a need for a faithful friend—a strong protector, always available, wise enough to solve any problem—God. Perhaps this is why many children accept Jesus as Lord during this time."[6]

The Discipleship Stage

The Discipleship Stage is an important time to ground children in their faith, teach them to pray, and help them to connect with God on a daily basis and learn to know him more. We don't want to leave them on the delivery table without spiritual care and nurturing!

Regular family devotional times can be significant discipling times, when you read God's Word aloud, discuss it in light of the real challenges and life experiences each person is facing, and pray together about concerns and for others. Christian activities with other children can also help your child grow in his relationship with God as the children fellowship, play, pray, and learn together. Realizing we belong to a community of believers that's bigger than "me, myself, and I" and that we're not "Lone Rangers" in the spiritual journey is a great support to a young person's faith.

What You Can Do: Making the Most of the Spiritual Window

Pray for Your Child

When our friends Melissa and Al were expecting their first son, John Paul, they prayed for him every night. They put their hands gently on Melissa's expanding abdomen and prayed that John Paul would come to know the Lord, love Jesus, and walk with him. They read Bible verses to him and sang to him. After he was born, they continued to surround him with prayer and spiritual awareness, praying specific Scriptures for him, holding hands with him at mealtime, praying at bedtime, thanking God throughout the day as something reminded them of his goodness.

When you pray for your child, it is helpful to pray scriptural prayers like:

I pray that _____ will know Christ in whom are hidden all the treasures of wisdom and knowledge and that they will be taught by the Lord, and great will be their peace. (Col. 2:3, Isaiah 54:13)

God, thank you that you will command your angels concerning your child to guard her in all her ways. (Psalm 91:11)

I pray that my children would walk in the fear of the Lord. As I trust you to teach them how to choose the best, keep them living within your circle of blessing. (Psalm 25:12–13)

An inexhaustible number of scriptural prayers and promises help us to pray in accordance with God's will. Seek his guidance and ask him to reveal his will for your children and how to pray for them—it's a prayer the Lord loves to answer! Not only pray for your children when you're alone and things are quiet, but let them hear you pray. If we want them to pray, they need to hear us pray for them. And then share the ways God answered and demonstrated his power and faithfulness. Praying for your child is like spreading a warm quilt of God's presence and love—it stores up blessings that will be showered upon your child at just the right time of need.

Capitalize on Your Child's Sense of Wonder

From wonder it's only a few steps to worship! Part of building an environment where kids can love and know God is seeing him in everyday life—how the rainbow is God's sign and promise, how the diversity of animals at the zoo shows God's creativity. When you're gardening, you can point out that without rain or watering from the hose in dry weather, plants wither and die—just like we dry up spiritually without the water of God's Word and presence.

Kids are naturally astonished at little things—bugs, butterflies, and clouds that are shaped like Barney. Taking time to stop and say, "Wow, God! You are awesome for giving us this sunny, perfect day to be at the park!" helps your child sense God's presence and learn gratefulness.

Teach Simple, Conversational Prayer

Encourage your child that prayer is not just for when he lies down to sleep, but he can pray anywhere, anytime, about anything, and God listens. God not only listens, he acts and shows us great things!

Share Jeremiah 33:3 where the Lord promises, "Call to me and I will answer you and tell you great and unsearchable things you do not know." Help your children to memorize short biblical prayers—"Help me trust in you with all my heart" (Proverbs 3:5) or "Create in me a . . . clean heart" (Psalm 51:10 LB).

Kids need to know that they don't have to pray long, eloquent prayers for God to hear them. And the best way to find that out is to hear you pray short, honest, from-the-heart petitions. Then they think, "I could talk to God like that!" and they grow in confidence in prayer. You can go on prayer walks where you walk around the block together, praying a blessing on each neighbor as you pass the houses, because children love praying while moving. You could put pictures of family and friends you want to remember to pray for in a basket on the dinner table.

As you ask God for creative ways to help kids connect with God, imaginative ideas often emerge. In a preschool, after the teacher had been praying about teaching the students to pray, the idea came for a "Jesus phone," a play telephone located in one of the learning centers.

As they were having circle time, the teacher said, "Shhhh," and then, "Oh, I hear something. . . . I think it's a ringing sound." After a few minutes, she went over to the phone and said, "Well, wouldn't you know—it's Jesus on the phone," and she asked the kids what they wanted to tell Jesus. Much conversation ensued. One preschooler told Jesus about being bitten by her puppy; another that he got hurt and could Jesus make it better; a third that he was lonely, that no one would play with him.

"It's incredible. They just want to 'talk' to him! And isn't that what prayer is about? Communication and relationship?" said the teacher.

Be Discerning

Be careful about the television shows, movies, computer and video games, magazines, and bedtime stories you bring into your home. Do these resources reflect God's values and build your child spiritually?

Teach Scripture

The verses your child learns throughout childhood are treasures that will yield benefits both now and later, sometimes sooner than you think! Julie, a Virginia mom, found that her son's repeating the Bible verse "Be humble, thinking of others as better than yourself" (Phil. 2:3 LB) until he knew it by heart was paying off.

While on vacation, Josh's seven-year-old sister, Becca, with whom he was in great competition, had been sick during the night and was having a difficult day. She'd had a major disappointment and was very teary and in need of compassion. Despite being preoccupied with a favorite activity, Josh noticed Becca's misery. He stopped what he was doing and whispered in his mother's ear, "Mommy, I know what Becca needs." He then gave his sister a generous portion of his candy (a treat from a vending machine). After getting over her shock at Josh's kindness, Becca was quite blessed by her brother's sacrificial gift!

Josh learned Scripture best by repeating the verses aloud. But some kids will memorize better by setting the verse to music or to a rhythmic beat, by reciting it while riding on a stationary bike or shooting baskets, or drawing a picture of the key words in the verse and having the words and picture on a card to look at often. Children retain Bible verses when they know what they mean, so first explain the meaning in a way they can relate to, and you will boost their memory.

Shower Your Kids with Blessings

Steve, a father of two, wanted to give his daughter a blessing as she was approaching the start of first grade. He called the family together, explained how this "would be a tradition that would continue for other milestones" in his children's lives, read the following blessing to Whitney, then presented a written copy to her:

MY DEAR WHITNEY,

Tomorrow is your first (major) step on your journey from being our chosen little baby girl to a beautiful unique young lady. Your mother and I are proud of you. We are proud of your external and internal beauty, your inexhaustible inquisitive spirit, your mothering instincts, your affectionate ways, and your quick mind that sees and hears everything.

Through Christ, our Lord, I bless you and pray God's blessings upon this step and throughout your life journey. I pray for self-discipline and excellent study habits, for balance and enjoyment of the journey, for lots of good friends, and, at the right time, a deep committed love like Mom and I have, and for a focus on relationships rather than things. . . .

Your mother and I are thankful that, out of the infinite combinations and possibilities, God chose you to be a part of His and our family forever and ever, Amen.[7]

This was the first of many blessings Whitney and her brother received on events—a sixteenth birthday, getting a driver's license, graduation from high school.

Make a "Worship Box"

A way to enliven family devotional and worship times is to make your own 3-D visual aids and put them in a special box, with enough of each kind for each family member to hold their own. Each child gets a turn to choose one, and then everyone sings the song that goes with the visual aid. For example, with little flags, they sing, "Joy is the flag flown high from the castle of my heart. . . ." With tiny sheep they sing, "The Lord is my shepherd." With bells, they join in on, "Praise Him, Praise Him, all ye little children, God is love. . . ." And Russian dolls go with "Jesus loves the little children. . . ."

A Pennsylvania family, the Hannays, found their children loved family worship because of the worship box. Before the kids could walk, they would eagerly crawl over as fast as they could when they saw Mom or Dad get out the worship box. The parents' prayer is that they will be able to continue to keep their children excited about their relationship with the Lord!

Start Family Traditions

Holidays are wonderful times to impart spiritual principles and truths to children. While trimming the Christmas tree, you can explain how the evergreen represents eternal life. When lighting candles you can explain that it's God's Light, Jesus, that came into the world at Christmastime. When Advent and Lenten devotional times and the traditions we celebrate for holidays are Christ-centered, we are impacting our children's lives for eternity.

Most of all, your loving care for your children will impart a sense of trust and security that makes it easy for them to love and trust their heavenly Father. And someday when you put their hand in his for the final time as they leave home for college or marriage, you will have given a lasting spiritual legacy for them to build on. They'll have Scripture verses God will bring back to their memories, hymns and praise songs tucked away, and a growing relationship with the Lord that will sustain them through both happy and difficult times ahead.

> **TIP:** To demonstrate God's love, as a family project fix up and deliver a Thanksgiving basket to a needy family.

Spiritual Window Closers to Avoid

Lecturing, pushing, convincing. Instead, help your children to see God's goodness in their lives and talk about him when they are struck by the wonders of nature around them or experiencing a moment of happiness. Make sure they're in an environment both at home and church that will help instead of hinder their knowing the Lord. Although we can't force them to drink, we can bring them to his living water!

Confusing kids about who God is. If you say God is angry at them because they acted foolishly or he's going to "get them" for an infraction, they'll see him as a punitive cosmic parent who is poised to catch them instead of a loving Father. Be cautious about what you say about God—kids believe you! Also, explain words like "under the blood" or "asking Jesus into my heart" and the words to hymns or praise songs they're singing. Don't assume they know what these phrases and other spiritual jargon mean.

Waiting to share your beliefs. Waiting until your children are older and able to decide for themselves before you share your beliefs wastes the opportunities of those early years. If you follow the route of not leading your children to an early knowledge of God and let them figure out spiritual matters on their own, you will have missed the greatest opportunity of a lifetime to build spiritual foundations in your children. God wants children to know him and he wants to show his love for them *now*.

Not walking your talk. Kids see through it so quickly when our "walk" with God doesn't match our "talk." If they don't see you giving generously and cheerfully to the Lord, how can they be expected to have that kind of attitude? If they don't see you reading your Bible or talking to God about your problems, how will they know that's important? Be a living example of the Golden Rule, of devotion and obedience to God, and you'll keep the Spiritual Window wide open in your child's life. And while you're "walking" with them, share stories of what God has done in your life, both in the past and the present. Constantly give him credit and acknowledge his faithfulness in your family life.

Underestimating children's spiritual potential. God also wants to use kids *now*, not after they've grown up, but often we don't give our children an opportunity to be used by God. They can impact their neighborhood by going on prayer walks, they can be a part of outreach and missions, they can start developing their own history with God by praying about their needs and seeing him work in their lives. Kids today have great spiritual capacity, just as David, Samuel, and Josiah did in biblical times. All we have to do is tap into it! We need to be sensitive to the contributions of children and recognize how we can involve them in prayer, outreach, and the life of the church—not just entertain them.

Failing to listen. We miss out on some of our best opportunities to share God's goodness with our children when we're too busy to listen. They are often asking insightful questions about God for which we don't have to have all the answers. But just listening to them is a gift that keeps their Spiritual Window open and greatly enhances their connection with God.

Letting busyness squeeze God and church out of our lives. When Sunday morning soccer takes precedence over church, when the chaos of the week means Sunday morning is only a time to sleep in, or we're always too busy for family devotions or prayer, then kids get the message that God is not a priority. But when they see faith in action, those attitudes shape their values. Also, do what you can to make Sunday morning extra positive so your children can learn by watching you "enter his gates with thanksgiving" (Psalm 100:4).

Spiritual Window Resources

"Step by Step: Leading Your Child to Christ," video by Art Murphy (Arrow Ministries, 407-859-9683).

"Tell Me About God: Helping Children Develop a Relationship with God," video (Paraclete, 800-451-5006).

"Prayerwalking for Kids," video (Fawn Parish, 805-987-0064).

"My Family's Prayer Calendar" (Ministry to Today's Child, 800-406-1011).

God's Children Pray by Dr. Mary Manz Simon (Concordia, available at Christian bookstores).

Praying the Bible for Your Children and *Praying the Bible for Your Baby* by Heather and David Copp (Colorado Springs: Waterbrook, 1998, available at Christian bookstores).

When Mothers Pray and *When Children Pray* by Cheri Fuller (Christian bookstores; Multnomah, 800-929-0910; or Cheri's Web site, www.cander.net/~cheri).

The following publish a huge variety of children's music resources to enhance your child's spiritual development: Integrity Music, 800-239-7000; Benson Music Group, 800-444-4012; Sparrow Corporation, 615-371-6800; and Nelson/Word, 800-933-9673.

*Lord, what an overwhelming responsibility it is
to spiritually parent my children!
You have provided this window of spiritual opportunity
in their young lives, so I ask you to equip me to make the most of it.
Since I can't give away what I don't have,
I pray for an increasingly close relationship with you,
for the wisdom to shepherd and guide my children into your arms,
and the humility to ask forgiveness when I fail.
Grant me the awareness to "see" moments when I can point them to you,
and help me to slow down to pray with and for my kids
so they'll always know they can turn to you.
Help us as parents to live before our kids in such a way so that they will
    be enticed to your banquet table!
May your love keep on growing more and more in us.*

Ten

the values window

THEODORE ROOSEVELT

When Carl, a Colorado dad, was involved in community service, he brought his children along and gave them opportunities to serve. Project Angel Tree, a Christmas ministry to prisoners' children, was a big project at their house. Carl had one of his daughters, when only five years old, help him select and sort gifts for the children. As his girls got older, he took them with him on the deliveries and to decorate and help with the party at their church for kids who had a parent in prison.

Since Carl feels that character is "caught" as much as "taught," he looked for opportunities like this to let his children be involved with all kinds of church, service, community, and household projects. As their involvement grew, Carl found their empathy and compassion for others grew and they began to initiate ideas on how to help others.

What this dad was doing was taking advantage of the golden opportunity of early childhood to impart values to his children. He wasn't just hoping that the church would do a good job of helping his kids develop a sense of right and wrong, of kindness and respect for others. He wasn't depending on the school to build a foundation of values and morality in his children, although he got involved in both institutions to make sure that the values being taught at home were being reinforced instead of contradicted at church and in school.

Carl was doing some of the most important work of parenting—using the time during his children's "Values Window" to build a solid foundation for behavior and decisions they'd make for a lifetime.

What Are Your Values?

Before talking about ways to shape our children's values and build their character, we first have to look at what values we hold dear. Politicians, teachers, the news media—everyone's been talking about *family values* lately. *Values* means whatever we judge worth

- **Being**—like happy, honest, successful, or physically fit.
- **Doing**—like helping others, reading, or competing and winning in sports.
- **Having**—like money and material things, peace and harmony, or a close family.

The first step in passing values to your child is to decide *what are the core or central values* you live by and those you want your child to understand and internalize as she grows—because even if you aren't conscious of it, you're imparting your values by how you live before your child.

Do you value honesty and hard work above everything else? Is a relationship with God at the top of what you want to pass on to your children? Everything we do is shaped by our values; our actions, behavior, and decisions are determined by our values. What is most important to you?

A good place to look when you're considering these "most important values" is the Bible. Absolutes are given in the Ten Commandments (contrary to modern opinion, not titled by God the "Ten Suggestions") and Galatians 5:22, which lists the fruits of the spirit of love, joy, peace, patience, kindness, goodness, faithfulness, gentleness, and self-control. Another good place to start is the book of Proverbs, which is full of descriptions of good and bad character traits.

Values such as respect for others and kindness, honesty, service, responsibility, work ethic, stewardship, perseverance, and determination are usually considered universal values. Experts agree that one of the most important values children will need as they enter the twenty-first century is faith. Faith is what gives a young person a sense of worth and purpose and helps him thrive and bounce back no matter what difficulties he faces.

After some reflection, write down eight to ten of the most important values you want to help your children integrate into their lives. Call the list "Our Family's Values." If you and your spouse disagree, discuss the differences so you can come to some agreement about what kind of "baton of values" you want to pass on to your kids.

Then, as you get ideas from this chapter, jot them down. From time to time get your family's value list out, jot down new ideas, and check to see how you're doing.

What We Know About Raising Moral Kids

The early years are "prime time" for moral development. While the shaping of morals and values continues throughout a person's life, most children begin to grasp the fundamentals during their first five years,[2] and much of their character will be formed by then. Just as you teach language and musical skills in the first years of a child's life, you teach moral and ethical reasoning in the first years of a child's life, during the Values Window—a golden opportunity when parents are the primary influence in their children's lives, a time when children are quite open to learning. Training in values and morality gets more difficult as children get older, but it is never too late.[3] Parents are the primary character teachers, and home is the place for kids to learn values.

Children have more capacity for having a sense of morality and a sense of what's right and wrong than we thought. Psychiatrist Robert Coles, author of *The Moral Life of Children*, says, "Children are capable of making moral distinctions even when they are as young as 5 and 6 and 7 years old." He says children have a sense of justice, try to figure out why things are the way they are, and identify with people who are suffering. If young children are given encouragement to ponder and discuss moral issues, he adds, then their moral life grows stronger.[4]

For decades, many psychologists thought that children couldn't act morally out of their own intrinsic motivation until post-adolescence. They thought children acted only from the fear of being punished or the expectation of being rewarded. They had rather low expectations for the moral development of children.

But just as we're discovering children are smarter and have more capacity for learning in the early years than previously thought, we're finding they have more capacity to learn and internalize good morals and values.

According to Michael Schulman, chairman of the Columbia University Seminar on Moral Education, there are some milestones for moral development:

By eight to eighteen months: By the age of eight to eighteen months, children develop an awareness that their actions can hurt people or make them happy. They begin to understand basic moral instructions like "Be gentle," when patting a younger baby.

By two to three years of age: Children can understand and empathize with other people's feelings and hurts, and respond by being kind (offering, for example, their pacifier or "blankie" to another child who is crying). Even before the age of two, kids can understand causal relationships (if I do this, then this will happen). They also begin to understand the abstract concept of fairness and respond to Mom's request to cooperate or exercise self-control.

By the age of three to four years: Children can recognize selfish behavior as wrong.

Age five and beyond: Starting at age five, children begin to think about moral judgments and are able to notice hypocrisy, or moral inconsistency, in adults. Five- and six-year-olds are able to share, comfort, and encourage others, and they understand the importance of respecting a person who looks or acts "different." These milestones of ethical development in children don't mean they've "arrived" in their values. On the contrary, kids can be inconsistent at times (especially when fatigued or under stress) and make us wonder if we've taught them anything about kindness—as when they verbally attack a sibling, reducing her to tears, or selfishly take all the best toys in the playroom.

Elementary and middle school: In the elementary and middle school years, children form their moral and religious identities, encounter their first ethical dilemmas (whether they should cheat when several students in their class are, or should they stick up for a handicapped child on the playground who's being made fun of). They develop attitudes about friendship, work, money, and whether it's worthwhile to be honest.[5]

Teaching Values

Values (like honesty, respect, kindness, responsibility, and religious beliefs) are best taught in the little moments: day-to-day experiences and activities at home, in habits we teach, in storytelling, in role-playing, and, most importantly, in parents' role-modeling, rather than in formal lectures or presentations. The number one way children learn anything is by watching and imitating the example of parents and important adults around them. They are observing parents all the time, so the best teaching mode for raising moral children is being a good example of the virtues and values you want your children to develop as they grow.

Two Key Factors

Relationship with parents is at the core of a child's moral motivation system, and it's a key to imparting virtue and character. Research shows that the two most important factors when teaching values by instruction or advice are the emotional bonding between parents and children and the parents' own behavior.[6] A morally responsible person, says Dr. Stanley Greenspan in *The Growth of the Mind,* grows out of the affectionate and secure family that is characterized by empathic, sensitive nurturing combined with clear, firm limits.[7]

What children observe in the relationship between their mother and father is a primary influencer of kids' value systems.[8] If parents treat each other in a loving way, children tend to treat their siblings, friends, and others with more love and caring.

Character counts! Although high IQ (Intelligent Quotient), EQ (Emotional Quotient), and creative thinking are important, a child with strong values and character will generally succeed more in school and life. In fact, according to John Rosemond, family psychologist and author of *A Family of Value*, a child with an IQ of 95 who is respectful, responsible, and resourceful will learn and achieve more than a child with an IQ of 165 who is deficient in those traits.[9]

> **TIP:** Let your child see you and your spouse express gratefulness to each other. Your example is a key to your child developing a thankful attitude.

Missing the Values Window

William Kilpatrick, author of *Why Johnny Can't Tell Right From Wrong*, tells a tragic story that illustrates the importance of the Values Window and what happens when we miss this window of opportunity.

An ancient king devised a wicked experiment to find out what language a child would speak if isolated from oral language and left to develop verbally on his own. The king commanded that two babies be taken away from their biological parents and raised by deaf-mutes. The infants were isolated from contact with speaking people or anyone else. What was the result?

Neither child learned to speak a word and, for their entire life, they both remained mute.[10]

This isn't just an experiment that took place in the Dark Ages, Kilpatrick goes on to explain. It also happened in America beginning in the 1960s when educators decided it was best to let children make up their own minds about what was right and wrong instead of imposing values on them. They began to teach and promote a relativistic value system with techniques like values clarification and decision-making instead of basing their behavior on absolute values.[11]

Just as in the king's day, the result has been disastrous. A whole generation of young people lost their moral compass—they're in a crisis so great that several years ago a commission of medical, educational, political, and business leaders, concerned about the problems of American children, met and published a report called "Code Blue," which warned that suicide is the second leading cause of death among adolescents, teen pregnancy has risen more than 621 percent in the last four decades, teen homicide has increased dramatically, and every year substance abuse is claiming younger victims.[12]

What You Can Do: Teaching Values

What's a parent to do in the face of these disturbing trends? I like what Dr. Thomas Lickona, author of *Raising Good Children*, says. "If children are to survive and thrive in this society, it's up to parents *to reclaim their authority and instill good values in their children at a very young age* (emphasis mine)."[13]

What can you as a parent do to reclaim your authority in this area? How can you instill strong values in your kids and raise them to be responsible, honest, compassionate, and respectful? The good news is you are the best person to build a solid moral foundation in your child, and you have the ideal values and character lab—your home!

A child with strong values isn't as vulnerable to peer pressure, develops more confidence that he can make a positive difference in the world, is less likely to abuse drugs or alcohol, is more likely to practice sexual abstinence, and is much better prepared for the challenges of life. Although many schools around the country are beginning to use values curriculums to teach good character, these values are no substitute for parents teaching values at home.

What your child learns from you has a long and powerful influence on your child's values. Your consistent example—being honest, thankful, kind, and working hard—can reinforce on a daily basis the importance of these values. And when you practice, discuss, and read about these values as part of your everyday routines of living together, you'll be fostering your child's growth in character.

The Trait of Perseverance

Let's take the character trait of perseverance to demonstrate a manageable way you can instill this and other values. Note that you can apply these steps or principles to any character quality or value you want your children to learn.

Why start with perseverance? Because it's a pretty important value. You can be super smart, but without perseverance—the ability to bounce back and keep going after failures and setbacks—you can't accomplish much in the real world. We'll look at how you not only teach the value of perseverance but help your child internalize it as well:

Loving Your Child

In chapter 2, "The Emotions Window," we pointed out the importance of children being loved and nurtured. The close, warm, loving relationship between parents and children is the beginning of the children's moral training and the cornerstone of character. Many studies show that kids who have felt secure and loved and whose needs have been met in the early years by a sensitive and accepting mother have an easier time loving others, being kind, obedient, and respectful, and following moral directions.[14]

Actions Speak Louder Than Words

Someone said, "Don't do anything at home that you don't want your children to do in public." That's because kids learn best by imitation, so modeling perseverance is the most powerful, positive tool you have when teaching your kids. For example, if you want your son to stay on the soccer team even though the team has lost every game of the season, let him observe you persevering on a difficult project at home or at work. Then, when you say, "I know your soccer team has had a rough season, but that's no reason to quit or miss practice. Hang in there," your message will have much more impact.

It's not that words aren't important, but when we say one thing and do another, it undercuts and confuses the message. For example, if you're trying to teach honesty, avoid calling in sick for work if you're not. If you're trying to help your child become responsible for his actions, don't blame the teacher when he flunks a test or race up to school to bring him an assignment he forgot and left at home. If you're encouraging him to "Just say no" to alcohol, do the same. And when you fail, as we all do, let your child see you take responsibility, and apologize when you're wrong.

Hands-On Values Lessons

Developing a value like perseverance is a lot like building muscles—it takes regular workouts and daily training. You could provide some "workouts" with long-term activities like gardening, which teaches perseverance in a fun way (growing pumpkins from seeds), or building over time a collection of stamps, coins, rocks and minerals, or anything else. When your child starts collecting things, help him organize them in shoe boxes, egg cartons, clear plastic bins, or albums instead of letting them turn into clutter. Adopting an elderly person in a nursing home whom you and your child faithfully visit each week, even when you don't "feel" like it, not only develops perseverance but a sense of compassion for others.

At the same time, decrease your family's television watching (which encourages quick fixes, easy thirty-minute answers to problems, and a very short attention span) and instead encourage projects like woodworking or crafts, making a book, working a 1,000-piece puzzle as a family, or writing and sending out a family newsletter periodically to extended family members.

Read Along, Read Aloud

My favorite ways to impart values to my children were through reading, everyday conversation, and storytelling. When these activities are happening right along with your positive role-modeling as you go about normal everyday activities, the values are reinforced in a pleasant, fun way.

Stories give us a sense of who we are and what values our family holds dear, even back a generation or two. Tell about times your grandfather kept farming in spite of crop failures and obstacles, or a time you kept trying at a job or task when you were tempted to throw in the towel.

Read aloud books about people who persevered in spite of difficulties and even tragedy. Here are a few who have.

- Eric Liddell, Olympic champion during the 1920s who consistently followed Christ even when that meant facing extreme danger and, ultimately, death in a Japanese prison camp.
- Amy Carmichael, who devoted her life to serving God in India despite incredible odds and founded the Dohnavur Fellowship.
- Joni Eareckson Tada, a quadriplegic as a result of a diving accident who turned personal tragedy into triumph. A creative artist, speaker, and writer, she has founded a ministry to the disabled—JAF Ministries.
- Dave Dravecky, a professional baseball player who survived cancer and amputation of his pitching arm, who gives hope to cancer patients all over the country.

Then there are a host of biblical people who persevered and have much to teach us—Noah, Abraham, Joseph, Paul, and those listed in the "Hall of Faith" in Hebrews, chapter 11.

In addition, classics like Harper Lee's *To Kill a Mockingbird*, Joseph Conrad's *Lord Jim*, and Dostoyevsky's *Crime and Punishment* show the consequences of good and bad behavior and offer an opportunity for your child's mental and moral development.

Quotes, newspaper clips, and wise sayings that relate to the values you are trying to teach your children are good to collect and post on the refrigerator to provide "food for thought."

Family conversation, whether at the dinner table, over cookies and milk, or in the car while traveling, provides many opportunities for sharing values. Use situations in everyday life as a springboard for talks on good character and values. When Mom gives money to a man holding a sign on the corner that says, "Please help me," and Dad says, "I think if the man put his efforts into finding a job, his family would be better provided for," then a lively discussion might occur. Mom and Dad can disagree respectfully but talk about moral issues and virtues, and perhaps even ponder, "What would Jesus do?" Young people who learn to talk about moral and ethical issues at home will be much better prepared to tackle the difficult decisions they will face in adulthood.

Focus on the Donut!

Last, while you're teaching the value of perseverance or any other virtue, don't forget to mix a regular dose of encouragement whenever you see your child's progress. Be sure to focus on his efforts and little steps of growth (the donut), not just the finished product or what he hasn't done properly (the hole). Kids are works in progress and rarely act perfectly all the time. When your child does show perseverance, say something about it: "You could have just quit when that puzzle got difficult, but you kept at it and I really admire your perseverance!" By commenting positively on your child's perseverance, you are nurturing that very quality.

You don't have to profusely praise everything he does, but it does help to catch your child being kind or responsible or making good decisions. Give him little snapshots of what he's becoming: "You gave your friend the biggest piece of cake even though it's your favorite. That's kindness in action," or "I really appreciate the way you helped your sister clean up her mess. You were showing such a serving attitude."

Whether it's teaching your children responsibility, or honesty, or respect, or courage, when you share your own beliefs and experiences, you are giving them one of the greatest gifts of all—a strong foundation of values.

What Values Are Being Taught at School?

While you are working on moral development at home, it is important to know what values are being taught in the classroom so that mixed messages aren't being given to your child. This is especially true since values are being taught as part of the curriculum of many schools. Besides the overt teaching of morals, many beliefs and values are subtly transferred in the teaching of science, social studies, literature, and other subjects. Find out what they are, first by observing classes before you enroll your child in a school, and then by knowing teachers, reading textbooks, and considering these questions:

- What character qualities is the teacher praising?
- What kind of person are the teacher, coach, and other adults who work with your child? Is this the kind of person you want your child to emulate?
- Consider the weight a textbook assigns to certain issues. Does it seem lopsided in its presentation of a subject? Does the author seem to have an agenda? If so, what? A textbook author's treatment of history or science can impact your child's view of the world.
- Be aware of the values depicted in stories and books you read or your child reads for school. Does the author portray the characters in the story with qualities you hope to develop in your child's life? What values does the "hero" live by? After reading a book, talk about the story and the character qualities highlighted.
- Overall, is what your child learns at school in line with or in conflict with what you're trying to teach her? If you're willing to take the time and effort, even omissions in schoolbooks (such as downplaying the role of motherhood or a biology book that omits creationism) can provide opportunities for you to discuss issues and read other resources with your child.

Become involved in planning character education in your community. Gather other parents and leaders to begin incorporating character education into schools and the community at large, teaching qualities such as good judgment, integrity and honesty, perseverance, responsibility, respect, self-discipline, and kindness—where adults don't just teach the values but live them out before students.

Developing Two R's and a G

Learning "Responsibility"

Children learn a sense of responsibility from pitching in on household chores. Even toddlers can pick up toys, dust furniture, make beds, and sort laundry (and at the same time develop motor skills, color skills, and sorting skills). Five- and six-year-olds can take their dishes to the kitchen and help load the dishwasher, contribute some of their savings to a charity, and assist in grocery shopping.

Responsibility is also developed when we let children experience consequences of their choices, set curfews and limits, and help our children set homework goals and then meet them. When your child has a big assignment looming, encourage him to write down a list of what needs to be done, assign each item on the list a priority number, and list steps to accomplish each task. And then do them. Such an approach teaches responsibility. Waiting until the night before the assignment is due and getting you (Mom or Dad) to do the project does not.

Raising "Respectful" Kids

Decide on specific words you don't allow in your home, and don't reward impudent or inappropriate expression. Set limits and firmly but warmly stick to them. You may have to periodically remind your kids who's in charge. I did, occasionally saying to a feisty child, "Ali, remember, I'm the mom."

Avoid overentertaining your kids because overprivileged, overstimulated children lose the ability to amuse themselves (while losing respect for the adults around them) and wail "I'm bored" at the first sign of a slowdown of entertainment.

Stirring Up "Gratitude"

At dinner every night, ask each family member to write a small note with a blessing received that day. Place the notes in a "Thankful Basket" in the center of the table. Then, once a week, read the notes aloud to remind everyone of the many good things that happen each day. While a grateful attitude can't be forced, as your children see you thanking your spouse and them and other people for kindness extended, they will more easily internalize a grateful attitude. Give each of your children a box of thank-you notes on Christmas and on birthdays, and then insist they write (even if your preschooler dictates the thank-you while you write the words) to Grandma and Grandpa, aunts, or friends to express appreciation for gifts received. Thank God together both at mealtimes and spontaneously through the day as you are aware of his goodness.

Chivalry isn't dead and neither are good manners. They disappear only when we don't expect them. From an early age, set high expectations for courtesy and manners in the family, things like saying "please" and "thank you," not interrupting others, teaching table etiquette, writing thank-you notes for gifts received, and especially speaking to your spouse and children just as politely as you want them to speak to you and others.

Values Window Closers to Avoid

Telling your kids "It's not your fault" while you rationalize and blame others, such as teachers, friends, or siblings, for problems.

Not having chores or responsibilities. Avoid doing your children's chores for them if they don't do their jobs, doing their homework, or redoing their tasks—because then they'll lack real reasons to grow more responsible.

Being a poor example or contradicting what you say with your actions. Those who have read this far knew I'd mention this window closer!

Allowing the world to revolve around your children with no limits or boundaries on their behavior. Overly permissive parents tend to raise young people who have a hard time with school, jobs, and life.

Not taking your children to church or sharing your religious beliefs and moral convictions.

Replacing time with your child for material things. It takes *lots* of time spent together to train a child in good manners and morals.

Character-Building Resources

William Bennett's *The Book of Virtues* (New York: Simon & Schuster, 1996), and *The Book of Virtues for Young People: A Treasury of Great Moral Stories* (New York: Simon & Schuster, 1996).

William Kilpatrick's *Books that Build Character: A Guide to Teaching Your Child Moral Values Through Stories* (including a listing of movies, available in video, that build good character) (New York: Simon & Schuster, 1994).

World-Proofing Your Kids: Helping Moms Prepare Their Kids to Navigate Today's Turbulent Times by Lael Arrington (Westchester, Ill.: Crossway, 1997).

Character Education Workbook by Judy Hoffman (a step-by-step process to help communities build a character-education program for their children) (Chapel Hill, N.C.: Character Development Group, 1997).

365 Ways to Develop Your Child's Values by Cheri Fuller (Colorado Springs: NavPress, 1994).

The Prince of Egypt Values Series: Moses Crosses the Red Sea, Miriam Watches Over Baby Moses, and *Moses and the Burning Bush* by Dr. Mary Manz Simon (Thomas Nelson, 1989; available at Christian bookstores).

Heavenly Father,
There are so many values I want my children to learn,
it can be overwhelming.
But since virtue and values start with me, I ask you
to work in me a godly character that would please you
and guide my kids in right behavior.
Strengthen my personal integrity,
and grant me the wisdom I so desperately need
to help my children develop solid values that will take them through
*   life.*

Eleven

understanding your child's individuality

Children in a family are like flowers in a bouquet: there's always one determined to face in an opposite direction from the way the arranger desires.[1]

MARCELENE COX

In the Griffin household, variety abounds, starting with the kids! Isaac, the firstborn, is very bright and very precise. At six he is detail-oriented; everything is black or white, no in-between. He follows directions closely and wants his siblings to do so too—he's everybody's policeman and can be bossy. Isaac isn't very active physically and often chooses reading or sitting and playing LEGOs rather than running in the yard like Noah, his brother. The older brother is just as cautious as the younger one is adventurous.

Isaac has a wonderful persistence when he starts a task. When he got an "Excavation Kit" for his birthday, he put on the plastic goggles, grabbed the hammer, and worked, worked, worked—not even stopping for a snack—at hammering away the sand in the kit until he reached his goal of retrieving the "skull" of a "dinosaur." His three-year-old brother, Noah, started hammering excitedly but got sidetracked playing in the sand. Isaac is predictable, whereas Noah is unpredictable. He's full of surprises! His mom isn't ever quite sure how he's going to respond to something.

Noah is more moody and wears his feelings on his sleeve. If he's in a bad mood, you know it, whereas Isaac is more controlled in his emotions. Not a strict rule-follower, independent Noah will start out to obey, but wants to do things on *his terms* and in *his way*. He's more active physically and better at athletics. If he makes something, it's with the purpose of flying it through the house or zooming around with it in the backyard. A strong auditory learner, if Noah hears something, he sings it, repeats it verbatim, and easily recalls it. His big brother is more visual in his learning style.

Little sister Elizabeth, 18 months, is the family "Mover," so they nicknamed her "Busy Bess." She talked earlier and talks much more than her brothers, is very social, and says "Hi!" to everyone she sees. Her interpersonal skills are already starting to bloom. Elizabeth is quite observant of what people are doing and tries to imitate the activity or task. She's also louder than her brothers and quicker to understand and pick up on things. She also has strong attachments to her favorite doll and stuffed animals and is her mom's delight (and sometimes, her brothers' frustration!).

Although all children have the same marvelous windows of opportunity we've been talking about as they grow, some will have more potential in certain windows—language or music may be one child's forte while physical prowess is another's strength—and we need to strike an important balance. Just as the children in the Griffin family are different, each child in your family, school, or church—in fact, each kid in the world—is unique. That means they have different temperaments, interests, bents, strengths, and weaknesses. Their talents and intelligence are also unique. God has wired each person differently and this affects their development. This means that although all children have a wide-open Music Window in the early years, some are going to progress faster in that area because of an innate musical intelligence, or giftedness. One of your children may show stronger language skills while another excels in art. While all kids' brains are being wired for logic and math thinking, as we saw in chapter 8, some will seem more accelerated in their critical thinking and numerical skills at an early age because that's their area of strength.

These strengths will affect how children respond to activities and resources, how fast they develop skills in a "window," and how they compensate in areas in which they are weak. So in addition to understanding the Learning Windows, it's vital for you to *know and understand your child*. In this chapter we're going to look at several aspects of knowing your child: temperament, learning style, and intelligence, or giftedness.

What We Know: Understanding Temperament

When our firstborn made his appearance in our family, I was trying to be a good mom while struggling with the normal tiredness and adjustments to the new role of parenting while trying to figure out our baby's cues. Justin was either extremely happy or intensely sad and let us know it! He tuned up every evening just as we were sitting down for dinner and wailed for no apparent reason. If we went to a new restaurant, he could be depended on to be fussy. He was determined, sensitive, strong-willed (all wonderful qualities, I discovered along the way).

Justin was an active baby who needed lots of *action* and *movement*, so I strolled with him what seemed like hundreds of miles his first year—in fact, we wore out two strollers. While he could be exuberant in familiar surroundings, he warmed up slowly to new experiences or people. For instance, in our YMCA mother-baby swim classes at nine months, he hated having his face in the water and didn't gurgle and play like his friend Gib. He wanted out of the pool pronto and was very verbal about his feelings on this. He wasn't like my friends' "easy," placid babies who willingly sat in their car seats during two hours of errands. Justin protested being confined and tried to figure his way out.

The Differences in Temperament

Was I doing something wrong? I often wondered until I found a wonderful resource, *Know Your Child* by Drs. Stella Chess and Alexander Thomas, which explains their perspective that from birth onward, babies vary in their behavior and their reactions to stimuli. In a twenty-five-year study that followed children from birth to adulthood (which has been confirmed by numerous other research studies around the world since the '50s when they began), Chess and Thomas found these temperamental differences aren't haphazard or vague, but in fact can be categorized into such specific traits as: activity level, rhythmicity, approach or withdrawal to new situations or stimulus, adaptability, sensory threshold, quality of mood, intensity of reaction, distractibility, persistence, and attention span. In each category, babies and older children can rate as mild or intense, high or low, quick or slow.[2]

Adapting Within the Parent-Child "Fit"

A key concept that Chess and Thomas discovered didn't focus on whether the child and parent were similar or whether the child had certain seemingly "ideal" or "easy baby" characteristics, but instead on:

- What kinds of demands are made on a particular child?
- What kinds of reactions does the child's behavior create in the parent?
- What kind of "fit" grew between parent and child?

The "goodness of fit" is what affected the child's progress the most and fostered his or her development and learning.[3] For example, they explain that a quick-moving, expressive parent might get very impatient and frustrated with a slow-moving, low-key child and even ignore the child's wishes since he expresses them so quietly. Or a parent who expects a low-adaptability child to quickly adjust and master new tasks can put demands on the child that the child simply cannot meet, thus bringing on a sense of failure and anxiety that causes the child to avoid future challenges.

As I read about the temperament traits, I began to realize that some of the "difficult" things I found in our child were related more to how different we were in temperament. I saw that what I was experiencing wasn't just because of my mistakes (although I made plenty of them). Some of the ways our child responded were *because of his own temperament*, because of how he was wired.

As I began to understand Justin's emotional patterns, I became more accepting of his intense emotions, more patient of his slow-to-warm-up approach to new situations, and more confident as a parent. I began to realize how his persistence and determination, as expressed when he was climbing out of a car seat or climbing to get something that was "off-limits" and trying *over and over again*, meant I needed to decide what the rules were and stick to my guns on the "majors" and safety issues and let some of the "minors" go. I also began to see this energy and persistence as a wonderful strength that would serve him well as he got older and even in school when he faced obstacles or needed to learn things that were difficult. I noticed ways to encourage Justin's individual temperament and strengths. As I did, the "goodness of fit" between me and our firstborn was greatly enhanced by my growing understanding.

As Justin has grown up (he's now 27 with a baby daughter of his own who doesn't like to be strapped in a high chair or car seat for long periods of time any more than he did), I've seen how his strengths are a vital part of his personality. His determination and persevering nature enabled him, right out of college, to earn fifteen business awards during the first year and a half of his advertising/marketing job for a communications company. Still active, he is training for a marathon. His sensitivity to how people are feeling strengthens his people skills. His strong verbal skills make him a terrific communicator, and his huge enthusiasm for projects or things he is interested in is contagious. He's a passionate person who has channeled his strengths productively as he's grown.

Clues to Temperament Traits

Let me briefly explain these temperament traits so you can better understand your child.

How active is your baby? How active your child is basically means the proportion of active and inactive periods. Does she kick and move about in the bathtub so much that you have to change your clothes afterward? Does your child love to climb, pull things out of drawers, race outside to play at the first opportunity, and usually select something *active* (like running or riding a bike) as opposed to a less active pastime like drawing or reading?

How predictable and consistent is your baby's behavior? This category of temperament is almost self-explanatory and relates to how predictable or unpredictable are your child's biological functions (hunger, sleeping and waking, bowel elimination). Some kids are quite predictable: they wake up at the same time, want to eat like clockwork, and go potty at the same time each day. Other children are much less predictable. Like Noah in the Griffin family, they are full of surprises.

How slowly or quickly does your child warm up to new situations? This refers to what kind of *first* response your child has to new situations or stimuli—a new person, place, food, plaything, or task to be learned. Does he spit out sweet potatoes the first time just because it's a new taste, cry when he sees a stranger, withdraw and clam up when moved to a new preschool class? He may be one of those kids who is slower in his "approach."

How flexible and adaptable is your child? This temperament trait has to do more with your child's *long-term* adjustment and flexibility to new or changed situations, beyond the first reaction. There is some overlap with the above trait of approach/withdraw. Our daughter Alison is a good example of slow adaptability. A delightful, exuberant child, Alison would not act like herself when she entered a new classroom; she did not have an easy time adjusting. We began to realize that although school started in September, it could take Ali until March or April to relax and really feel comfortable and be herself. But once she did, she'd begin to bloom and enjoy the environment and the people.

How sensitive is your child to sudden sounds, textures, and other sensory stimuli? This relates to the intensity level of stimulation it takes to get a response from a child—negative or positive. Some babies wake up if they hear a small sound in the room next door, startle easily, cry if they are wet, complain about the texture of their clothes as preschoolers, and are very sensitive to smells and other sensory stimuli—they would be described as having a low sensory threshold. For other children, it takes much more discomfort, sound, or other stimuli before they react.

Is your child's mood usually positive or negative? Some children seem to wake up after naps or a night of sleep in a joyful, pleasant mood, while others immediately cry and fuss upon awakening. The jollier temperament child will be the one who later sees the cup "half full," and the child with the more negative or melancholy mood sees it as "half empty," whether it's a party or school problem she's describing.

Our second-born son, Chris, is a good example of a child with a consistently positive mood. He woke up happy and went to bed the same way, unless sick. A rather quiet child, he was observing his surroundings all the time, entertained himself, rarely ever cried, and had a precious perpetual smile on his face unless something really bad happened. Fairly laid back about life, he did, however, begin to assert himself with his big brother and others around the age of three, as if to say, "Look out, world! I'm here and I have opinions too!"

How intense is your child in expressing reactions to situations? How intense is your child's response to frustrations or situations? A high-intensity child is like our firstborn, who either laughed enthusiastically or cried loudly—in either case, we knew exactly how he felt. A low-intensity child is more laid back about her emotions; she may fuss when upset about something, but you have to listen and stay tuned in to not miss her signals or you'll ignore needs.

Is your child easily distracted or very focused? Chess and Thomas described this trait as "the effectiveness of an outside stimulus in interfering with or changing the direction of the child's ongoing behavior."[4] That means if our son Justin wanted his bottle, nothing would distract him from his goal; he was highly focused, even as a baby. His brother, Chris, also was and is very focused and hard to distract. If he was building with LEGOs, he didn't want to stop until he was through with his project. Our daughter, Alison, was a bit more distractible; if she was doing homework, it took her longer because she was easily sidetracked—although it might be a wonderful drawing or batch of cookies she whipped up in the meantime!

What kind of attention span and persistence level does your child have? Somewhat related to distractibility, these two traits figure in strongly in learning and school issues. A child with low persistence starts working addition problems, and if she gets frustrated with the first few, she tends to give up. A child with high persistence keeps trying, even when facing obstacles, and doggedly works through the sheet of math problems until done, pestering anyone nearby for help if it's needed to complete the task.

With all the children labeled "attention deficit" these days, we're familiar with the child with a short span of attention—he's only interested in an activity for a short time and dashes off to pursue something else. While this can be due to a neurological problem, Chess and Thomas found the length of the attention span is also a temperament trait.

Certain of the temperament traits combine to produce a behavioral style they called an "easy" child (about 40 percent of kids studied), a "difficult" child (about 10 percent), or a "slow-to-warm-up" child (about 15 percent of the children).[5]

Remember, it's not whether kids are easy or difficult. How children do over the long run, as I explained above, has more to do with the personality or temperament "fit" between parent and child than it does with a certain type of personality in the child.

What You Can Do: Celebrating the Differences of Temperament

What is most striking to me as I've parented our own children and worked with many others is how what *looks* like a negative characteristic in childhood becomes one's greatest strength as an adult. A very active child can run his mom ragged (especially if she has a low activity level), but as an adult that same person has tremendous physical and mental energy and is extremely productive. The child with a seemingly melancholy mood develops into an artistic adult who achieves greatly in creative arts. The argumentative child who always challenges you and asks "why" becomes a top physics student. Your bossy child develops leadership skills that could enable her to be a CEO for a large corporation, serve as principal of a school, or become a senator. The super-persistent kid who kept poking at the electric outlets until you thought you were going to tear your hair out becomes the million-dollar salesman and marketing director of a large corporation. And the emotional child with high-intensity reactions becomes a very expressive actress.

Understanding your child's temperament can free you to accept her and celebrate her personality instead of bemoaning how different she is from you or her siblings. It can enable you to have realistic, though high, expectations for your child, and remove a lot of the stress from the parent-child relationship.

What We Know: Learning Styles

Another way children are wired differently is what we call "learning style," or how they process and learn information. This processing style affects how they interact with their world.

Seeing

Some kids have a natural talent for visual learning (learning through seeing, reading, and studying charts or diagrams), which helps them excel in areas like spelling, puzzle-working, and geometry. These "Looker" kids have a sharp memory for things they see, almost like a photocopy machine in the brain. Thus, it's easy for them to memorize what they read (just take a "picture" of it). These children tend to have a good sense of direction even when they're very young.

Listening and Talking

Other kids learn better auditorially (through listening and talking). I call these children "Talkers and Listeners" because although they're happy to listen to someone else (like the teacher), what they really like to do is express themselves! Their gifts cause them to do well in areas like following oral instructions, interacting in group discussions, and learning to read phonetically. It's as though the auditory learner has a tape recorder in his head taking in and storing sounds and words, important and not-so-important information.

Touching and Moving

Still other children have a talent for learning kinesthetically and tactilely (through movement and touch). These "Movers and Doers" seem to have a special control tower or computer that regulates and times their movements into a special rhythm or coordinated pattern. Movers learn best by doing. They often excel in athletics, mechanics, dentistry, engineering, and even brain surgery. Some kids are a blend of styles—a combination of visual, auditory, or kinesthetic strengths—and weaknesses. You might have an imaginative, visually strong learner who has trouble following oral instructions, a talented little soccer player who has difficulty with reading, or a child who is creative in visual arts but has a hard time handling symbols (such as those used in chemical formulas or algebra equations).

Even at the preschool stage, you can see children's emerging learning style and temperament by their likes and dislikes. They're starting to find out what they're good at, what they enjoy doing, and what they find stimulating or frustrating. A kinesthetic learner or mover finds he can climb on anything and ride a bike earlier than any other kid in the neighborhood, but gets frustrated with puzzles and decides he dislikes them. His visual learning sister finds she excels at puzzle-working and wants to do more. Another preschooler (an auditory learner) has a preference for word play and delights in listening to and telling stories. Observing the activities children like and dislike helps you understand learning style strengths.

What You Can Do: Maximizing Learning Style

When you understand your child's learning style, you increase the likelihood of your child learning to read well (by making sure his primary learning style is part of the early reading process) and can eliminate much of the homework conflict that arises once kids are in school. You can help your children develop study strategies that work for how they are wired and how they learn best, and you'll have the tools to help them become active learners (and even do chores and follow directions around the house as well). Try strategies like these:

The Looker (Visual Learner)

Provide lots of maps, diagrams, and charts. Give opportunities to draw, paint, and build with a variety of materials. Use visual objects to represent abstract ideas or concepts. Make an illustrated time line to learn history dates and events (with picture and date). Color-code highlighted information in books. Avoid disorganization because visual learners are easily distracted by clutter: too many articles tacked on the board or in the room, and it's harder to concentrate on the task at hand.

The Listener and Talker (Auditory Learner)

Provide lots of opportunities for storytelling, conversation, books on tape, and music. Create opportunities for writing to a pen pal, keeping a journal, and other writing activities. When material needs to be mastered for a test, quiz orally or use a fill-in-the-blank tape for review. Have your child play a card game like "Concentration" in which pairs of study cards are turned face down and then correctly matched as the game progresses (works well in foreign languages and even studying geography). Set information to a song or make an acrostic, using the first letters of the words to form a new word as a memory aid. Play the "Memory" game to develop visual memory skills. Encourage a study group where they orally go over the material, then the students make out ten questions they think the teacher will ask on the test, and they take the practice quiz.

The Mover (Kinesthetic Learner)

Buy a large white board with markers for your child to practice spelling words and math problems and to "teach" you information that he'll be tested on at school. Encourage lots of drawing in preschool years and let your child dictate stories and make them into "published" books. Make use of multisensory reading and writing materials (like sand on a cookie sheet to trace letters). Use items found around the house, like beans and muffin cups, for your mover to count, add, subtract, and multiply in a hands-on way. Allow your active child to bounce a basketball, clap his hands, or march around the room while practicing rote material like math facts. Make up a cheer for spelling words; remember that a mover can retain information better if it is set to song and movement.

Don't Forget the Weaknesses

While giving your child study techniques like those above that maximize his strengths, it's important to help him work on and compensate for his weaknesses. For example, Lookers need to develop good listening and communication skills and to learn to take good notes in class. A student who has visual strengths but whose auditory memory is weak may need an outline to keep up with an oral presentation. A Mover with a short attention span needs to increase his concentration and on-task focus. One way to do that is to regularly work together on a small project from start to finish. Just fifteen minutes of doing and focusing on one thing (while setting an egg timer)—putting together a puzzle, making a simple craft—will help develop the ability to focus in the classroom.

Recognizing how a child learns best and tapping into that is a great boost to the development of any child. When we highlight the positives (what the child can do well, what he's good at, and what he's interested in) rather than the negatives (his slowness in math or reading, his weak auditory memory), we help the child to compensate for his weaknesses and develop confidence in his strengths. As those strengths are recognized and reinforced, he gains momentum and is more motivated to tackle challenging tasks at school and keep on trying in spite of obstacles.

When you understand your child's strengths, you can help prevent learning problems. Since almost half of all kids in the average classroom experience some learning differences, it should be our goal to figure out how each child is wired. Besides, the top achievers are those students who realize what their strengths are and use those strengths when they study or have new or difficult information to learn.

What We Know: Recognizing a Child's Talents and Gifts

Understanding and knowing your children also means recognizing their individual talents and gifts, or how they are "smart." Sometimes it appears that the only kids considered "smart" are those who make good grades on tests and report cards. Actually, that's "school smart"—or usually a combination of language and math (or analytical) talent. And it's great for your child to have! This kind of "smart" helps kids bring home report cards and get academic awards at school assemblies that make you burst with pride.

But "school smart" isn't the only kind of "smart"; there are many "gifted" children who don't score high on pencil-and-paper tests. Most children have a natural talent in one or more areas. In fact, research shows that each one can do something better than 10,000 other people *if* their talent is discovered and developed. Now that's what I call "gifted"! Here are some of the ways kids are smart:

Language Smarts

Language and verbal ability, a sensitivity to the meaning and order of words as possessed by poets, writers, and speakers (think Robert Browning, Dr. James Dobson, Jane Austen). Kids who are fascinated with word play, rhymes, limericks, and such are natural storytellers or are imaginative with words.

Math Smarts

Ability in math, reasoning, and logical systems of thought like physics and chemistry. René Descartes, Stephen Hawking, and Sir Isaac Newton came by this kind of smart naturally. If your child has an intuitive skill with numbers or is argumentative and is always analyzing things, this may be one of his talents.

Musical Smarts

Has your child been able to remember and repeat tunes from the time she was small? Is she attracted to and fascinated by sounds? Does she play a musical instrument by ear? Does she have perfect pitch? If so, she probably is musically talented. So was Mozart!

Interpersonal, or People, Smarts

These are the skills that leaders like Dr. Martin Luther King Jr., senators, and corporate executives have, but you also need people skills to be successful in careers from sales to health care to diplomacy. This "smart" means the ability to understand people and how to lead, work, and communicate with them. In children, this is often a verbal child who is sensitive to others' feelings, has lots of friends, and is able to lead other kids on the playground to build a fort or do a project.

Body Smarts

Physically, or kinesthetically, smart children shine on the athletic field, in dance programs, sculpting classes, or in mechanical, computer, or other hands-on endeavors. Olympic divers, NBA basketball stars, actors, artists, and even neurosurgeons have this kind of smart. Does your child have excellent coordination, move his body with grace and timing, or manipulate things with lots of skill, dexterity, and precision?

Spatial Smarts

Wow, I love this kind of smart! These kids are able to visualize an object in their mind's eye and even imagine how it would look if it were turned around. They notice visual details, usually love to draw, and can see something once and reproduce it on paper. This creative child could become a great architect or artist, but wouldn't necessarily score high on pencil-and-paper tests and thus may not be termed "smart" at school. Spatial talent is seen in Mary Englebrit, an outstanding greeting card designer; Frank Lloyd Wright, the architect; and Dr. John Sabolich, an inventor of prostheses for amputees who has created limbs to help them dance, run, and even sky dive.

Intrapersonal, or Self-Awareness, Smarts

This is the somewhat inward, reflective child blessed with a sensitive awareness of his thoughts and feelings who often enjoys independent study and research. If your child is self-disciplined, insightful, and decisive, she may possess this kind of smart—which poets like William Wordsworth, psychologists like Carl Rogers, and theologians like Walter Wangerin share.[6]

What You Can Do: Developing a Child's Talents

Parents should keep in mind four important thoughts when considering a child's talents.

One, even at a young age you can recognize the different ways your children are talented. People with strong interpersonal skills are empathetic and good communicators even as young children. The kinesthetically smart little ones use their bodies to solve problems. Preschoolers who have a passion for drawing, building, and making things may be showing a strength in the spatial intelligence area.

A young artist in California is a good example. Eleven-year-old Alexandra has already created more than 350 paintings, and some have sold for as much as $125,000! When did Alex get her start? At the age of two she started coloring, painting, and drawing. If she could, she'd paint all day. She's now cut back to only three hours a day. She paints not to make money but because she loves to paint. Her role model is none other than Pablo Picasso!

Musically smart children can also be identified early. Usually when they start learning to play an instrument, they don't have to be reminded to practice—they beg for chances to play. Elizabeth, an eight-year-old New Yorker I met this summer, sang all the time. Her mom, MacBeth, said Elizabeth was almost "born singing." At the age of three, her parents started her in Suzuki violin lessons. In the first months of lessons, Elizabeth learned to play half of the first book; by Christmas break, she played everything with such skill that the director of the program took over her instruction.

Sometimes Elizabeth practiced three hours or more by her own choice. "She would pick up the violin on cold winter days and walk around the house playing. It was her second voice," said MacBeth. This eight-year-old, who can play anything she hears, has an extensive repertoire. First principal violin in her first children's orchestra, Elizabeth is being considered to play at Carnegie Hall this year. That's very special music talent!

Two, be aware that seemingly "negative" qualities may come with the package of smarts. A behavior that may be very irritating to you could be a marker or sign of your child's special "smarts." For example, when Thomas Edison was a child and saw his first bird's nest full of eggs, he was so excited and so intent on imitating the birds, he sat right down on the nest and smashed all the eggs. Fortunately, he had a patient mom, a mom to whom he later attributed his success.

Wade, a talented computer systems expert I know, dismantled a remote-control car he got one Christmas. When his mother's toaster wouldn't pop the toast up he took that apart (he did manage to fix the toaster). Wade was a terrific swimmer, fidgety when he had to sit for long periods at his desk, and was assigned to the slow reading group in second grade. But he discovered his strengths and has forged a wonderful career.

Three, use your child's "smarts" when she is trying to learn something. If she doesn't grasp the lesson in a language way, she may understand it more clearly through music or movement. If she doesn't understand a math assignment from the textbook's explanation, use a visual method (draw a picture) or a hands-on activity with items she can touch and move to understand the concept.

And four, being aware of these differences can help us to accept our children—their strengths and weaknesses—and nurture rather than squelch their God-given talents and gifts.

In each "window of learning" we've explored—music, language, curiosity, creativity, math and logic, etc.—all children have some potential to develop in these different learning windows of opportunity. And certain children are going to shine—depending on their strengths.

TIP: Follow your child's interests, whether map-making or art or music or writing or running a little business.

Resources to Develop Your Child's "Smarts"

Spatial Smarts

- Provide markers, paper, charcoal, brushes, easel, and other art materials.
- Provide games like chess, checkers, and computer graphics software.
- Encourage projects like assembling models of airplanes or rockets and inventing things.

Musical Smarts

- Provide rhythm instruments and chances to sing, clap, and play along.
- Play a variety of good music at home and in the car, including classical, folk, traditional kids' music, and the best Broadway scores.
- With a home computer, there are software programs designed to help your child to write and perform original music.
- Take your child to symphony concerts and live musical theater.

Body Smarts

- Find a physical activity your child enjoys and can develop skill in—individual sports, team sports, dance.
- Provide things to take apart (old clocks, electric toys from garage sales) and a toolbox with pliers, screwdrivers, and other tools.
- Provide opportunities to see a variety of athletic events in the community, from dance recitals to horseback riding competitions and swim meets.

Math and Logic Smarts

- Provide hands-on science projects and experiments, from stargazing in the backyard to collecting different kinds of insects.
- Play games like Mastermind, Battleship, chess, and Monopoly that require strategy and problem-solving.
- Read biographies about scientists and their discoveries.
- Watch TV specials on oceanography, space, aviation, and other science topics.
- Take advantage of summer math and science programs for children offered at colleges and universities around the country.

Language Smarts

- Make books out of stories your little storyteller tells you. Encourage making original greetings cards, writing play scripts to perform with friends, writing newsletters.
- Play word games like Scrabble, Password, Scattergories, and charades; make up rhymes, limericks, and tongue twisters.
- If your child writes a promising poem or story, help her submit it to a children's or teens' magazine for publication.

People Smarts

- Put your child in charge of a project such as planning a family camp-out or birthday party or helping with a neighborhood block party.
- Encourage your child in speech, debate, and student government activities at school.

- Suggest starting a little business: dog watching, a lemonade and brownie stand, or lawn mowing.

Intrapersonal Smarts

- Give your child opportunities to pursue his own special interests with magazines, field trips, and books.
- Encourage independent research, experiments, and personal projects.
- Encourage your child to keep a notebook or journal about his learning and thinking.

Lord, I'm grateful for the way you made
each member of our family unique and precious,
each one for a distinct purpose and destiny.
Besides, the fact that we're all different
makes life interesting and fun.
Having the ability to recognize and accept each child's uniqueness,
to know and understand them but not compare them,
to be positive even when things seem negative,
is a challenge only you can equip and enable me for.
So I'm grateful in advance for your divine help.

notes

chapter two: the emotions window

1. Jane Healy, in *Your Child's Growing Mind* (New York: Doubleday, 1987), 86.

2. J. Madeline Nash, "Fertile Minds," *Time* (February 3, 1997), 53.

3. Rima Shore, *Rethinking the Brain: New Insights into Early Development* (New York: Families and Work Institute, 1997), 39.

4. Daniel Goleman, *Emotional Intelligence* (New York: Bantam, 1995), 195.

5. Shore, *Rethinking the Brain*, 42.

6. Goleman, *Emotional Intelligence*, 192.

7. Shore, *Rethinking the Brain*, 27.

8. Ibid., 34–35.

9. Linda J. Heller, reporting in "Bulletin," *Parents* (June 1998), 105.

10. B. Renken et al., "Early childhood antecedents of aggression and passive-withdrawal in early elementary school," *Journal of Personality*, 57 (2) (1989), 257–81.

11. Robert Lewis, *Rocking the Roles* (Colorado Springs: NavPress, 1992).

12. Thomas Lickona, *Raising Good Children* (New York: Bantam, 1994), 47.

13. T. Berry Brazelton, *Heart Start: The Emotional Foundations of School Readiness* (Arlington, Va.: National Center for Clinical Infant Programs, 1992), preface, 7.

14. Stanley I. Greenspan, *The Growth of the Mind: And the Endangered Origins of Intelligence* (Reading, Mass.: Addison-Wesley, 1997), 311.

15. Ross Campbell, *How to Really Love Your Teenager* (Wheaton, Ill.: Victor, 1981).

16. Ibid.

17. Sarah Van Boven, "Giving Infants a Helping Hand," *Newsweek Special Issue* (1997), 45.

18. Henry Cloud and John Townsend, *Boundaries* (Grand Rapids: Zondervan, 1992), 41.

19. My thanks to Barbara Sorrell for sharing with me her understanding of praying through the developmental stages of a child's life.

chapter three: the creativity window

1. Roman Brown and Ramsey Brown, *101 Ways Kids Can Spoil Their Parents* (Bloomington, Minn.: Garborg's, 1998).

2. *People Magazine* (March 23, 1998), 71.

3. Teresa Amabile, quoted in Daniel Goleman, Paul Kaufman, and Michael Ray, *The Creative Spirit* (New York: E. P. Dutton, 1992), 57.

4. Ibid., 58.

5. Goleman, Kaufman, and Ray, *The Creative Spirit*, 59.

6. Jane Healy, *Your Child's Growing Mind* (New York: Doubleday, 1987), 333.

7. Ibid., 334.

8. Amy Nappa, *Imagine That! 365 Wacky Ways to Build a Creative Christian Family* (Minneapolis: Augsburg Fortress, 1998).

9. Mary Englebreit, "If You Can Dream It," *Guideposts* (October 1998), 7–9.

chapter four: the curiosity window

1. Dorothy Corkille Briggs, *Your Child's Self-Esteem* (New York: Doubleday, 1975), 263.

2. Gloria Latham, "Fostering and Preserving Wonderment," in *Australian Journal of Early Childhood*, 21, no. 1 (January 1996), 12.

3. From a personal interview with Dr. Jane Healy, author of *How to Have Intelligent and Creative Conversations with Your Kids* (New York: Doubleday, 1994).

4. From a personal interview with Dr. David Elkind, a professor at Tufts University.

5. Latham, "Fostering and Preserving Wonderment," 13.

6. From an interview with Darrel Baumgardner.

7. Jane Healy's book *How To Have Intelligent and Creative Conversations With Your Kids* is full of playful ponderings like these that stimulate curiosity and creative thinking.

8. Mildred Goertzel and Victor Goertzel, *Cradles of Eminence: A Provocative Study of the Childhoods of over 400 Famous Twentieth-Century Men and Women* (New York: Little Brown, 1962).

9. From an interview with Dr. Stanley Greenspan.

10. Richard Anderson et al., Becoming a Nation of Readers: The Report of the Commission on Reading (Champaign, Ill.: Center for the Study of Reading, 1988).

chapter five: the physical window

1. James C. Dobson, quoted in *Draper's Book of Quotations for the Christian World*, ed. Edith Draper (Wheaton, Ill.: Tyndale, 1992), 1107.

2. My appreciation to Kay Davis, pediatric physical therapist at Mercy Hospital in Oklahoma City, Oklahoma, for her consultation and suggestions on this chapter.

3. Sharon Begley, "Your Child's Brain," *Newsweek* (February 19, 1996), 61.

4. Ibid.

5. Ibid., 30.

6. From a personal interview with Dr. Richard Cotton of the American Council on Exercise.

7. From correspondence with researchers.

8. "Brain Needs to Rest to Store New Skills," PT Bulletin (September 19, 1997), 15.

chapter six: the music window

1. Edith Draper, ed., *Draper's Book of Quotations for the Christian World* (Wheaton, Ill.: Tyndale, 1992), 7930.

2. Vadim Prokhorov, "Will Piano Lessons Make My Child Smarter?" *Parade* (June 14, 1998), 18.

3. From an interview with Dr. Edwin Gordon, Temple University.

4. John Feierabend, "Music in Early Childhood," *Symposium on Early Childhood Arts Education* (July/August 1990), 15–20.

5. From an interview with Dr. Gordon Shaw, University of California.

6. From an interview with Dr. John Feierabend, Hartt School of Music, Hartford, Conn.

7. Donna Brink Fox, *Music Educator's Journal* (January 1991), 43–44.

8. Ibid., 43.

9. John Holt, *Learning All the Time* (New York: Holt, 1989), 114.

10. Prokhorov, "Piano Lessons," 14.

chapter seven: the language window

1. Gladys Hunt, *Honey for a Child's Heart* (Grand Rapids: Zondervan, 1969), 14.

2. Jeff Myers, *From Playpen to Podium* (Gresham, Ore.: Noble, 1996).

3. "The Amazing Minds of Infants," *LIFE* (July 1993), 52.

4. Geoffrey Cowley, "The Language Explosion," *Newsweek* Special Issue (Summer 1997), 16.

5. Shannon Brownlee, "Baby Talk," in *U.S. News and World Report* (June 15, 1998), 48–50.

6. Ibid., 50.

7. Ibid.

8. "The Amazing Minds of Infants," in *LIFE* (July 1993), 52.

9. Cowley, "The Language Explosion," 16–22.

10. Ibid.

11. Myers, *From Playpen to Podium*, 20.

12. Cowley, "The Language Explosion," 16.

13. Sharon Begley, "Your Child's Brain," *Newsweek* (February 19, 1996), 57.

14. Lucy Calkins, *Raising Lifelong Learners* (Reading, Mass: Addison-Wesley, 1997), 9.

15. Richard C. Anderson et al., *Becoming a Nation of Readers: The Report of the Commission on Reading* (Champaign, Ill.: Center for the Study of Reading, 1985).

16. Priscilla Vail, *Smart Kids With School Problems* (New York: E. P. Dutton, 1987), 164.

17. Ibid., 92–93.

18. Ibid.

19. Jane M. Healy, *Endangered Minds* (New York: Simon & Schuster, 1990), 86.

20. John Rosemond, "Speech Therapist Tests TV Theory on Daughter," in "Family Matters," "Accent" section, *The Sunday Oklahoman* (November 30, 1997), 5.

21. Thomas Armstrong, *Awakening Your Child's Natural Genius* (New York: Tarcher Putnam, 1991), x.

chapter eight: the math and logic window

1. "Math," *Life Magazine* (July 1993), 50.

2. Thomas Armstrong, *Awakening Your Child's Natural Genius* (New York: Tarcher Putnam, 1991), 75.

3. Rima Shore, *Rethinking the Brain: New Insights into Early Development* (New York: Families and Work Institute, 1997), 71.

4. John Holt, *Learning All the Time* (Reading, Mass.: Addison-Wesley, 1989), 100.

5. Barry J. Wadsworth, *Piaget's Theory of Cognitive and Affective Development* (New York: Longman, 1989), 25.

6. "Cultivating the Mind," *Newsweek* Special Issue (1997), 39.

7. Margie Golick, *Deal Me In: The Use of Playing Cards in Teaching and Learning* (New York: Monarch Press, Simon & Schuster, 1981), 22, 9.

8. Theresa and Frank Caplan, *The Early Childhood Years: the Two to Six Year Old* (New York: Bantam Books, 1983), 125.

9. Ibid., 362.

10. Jane Healy, *Your Child's Growing Mind* (New York: Doubleday, 1989), 302–3.

11. "Cultivating the Mind," *Newsweek*, 31.

12. Healy, *Your Child's Growing Mind*, 304.

chapter nine: the spiritual window

1. Corrie ten Boom, *In My Father's House* (Grand Rapids: Fleming H. Revell, 1976), 23–24.

2. Karen Henley, *Child-Sensitive Teaching* (Cincinnati: Standard, 1997), 51.

3. Ibid., 32.

4. David Walters, *Kids in Combat* (Macon, Ga.: Good News Fellowship Ministries, 1997), 46.

5. Sybil Waldrop, *Guiding Your Child Toward God* (Nashville: Broadman, 1985), 40.

6. Henley, *Child-Sensitive Teaching*, 56.

7. Children Are a Heritage from the Lord, A Nursery Handbook for Parents (Oklahoma City: Our Lord's Community Church).

chapter ten: the values window

1. Source unknown.

2. Michael Schulman, quoted in David Ruben, "How to Raise a Moral Child," *Parenting 10th Anniversary Issue* (Fall 1997), 66.

3. Michael Schulman and Eva Medler, *Bringing Up a Moral Child.* (Reading, Mass.: Addison-Wesley, 1985), 10.

4. "The Best Parents Learn from Their Children," Inquiry, *USA Today* (May 5, 1986), 13A.

5. Schulman and Medler, *Bringing Up a Moral Child*, 52–54, 234–37.

6. Henry Holstege, "Teach Them Well," in *Christian Home & School* (January 1987), 15.

7. Stanley I. Greenspan, *The Growth of the Mind: And the Endangered Origins of Intelligence* (Reading, Mass.: Addison-Wesley, 1997), 195.

8. Paul Lewis, *40 Ways to Teach Your Child Values* (Wheaton, Ill.: Tyndale, 1985), 88.

9. John Rosemond, "Three R's More Important Than IQ in Learning," in *The Sunday Oklahoman*, Accent Section (March 7, 1993), 10.

10. "Why Johnny Can't Tell Right from Wrong," in *Teachers in Focus* (June 1993), 6.

11. Ibid.

12. Dan Coats, "America's Youth: A Crisis of Character," in *Imprimis*, 20, no. 9 (Hillsdale, Mich.: Hillsdale College, September 1991), 1–2.

13. Thomas Lickona, quoted in Laura Sessions Stepp, "Raising a Moral Child," in *CHILD* (January 1993), 130.

14. Schulman and Medler, *Bringing Up a Moral Child*, 215–17.

chapter eleven: understanding your child's individuality

1. Edith Draper, ed., *Draper's Book of Quotations for the Christian World* (Wheaton, Ill.: Tyndale, 1992), 6227.

2. Stella Chess and Alexander Thomas, *Know Your Child* (New York: Jason Aaronson, 1996), 63.

3. A good resource for parents who want to explore this topic more is a book by Stella Chess and Alexander Thomas, *Goodness of Fit: Clinical Applications from Infancy Through Adult Life* (Philadelphia: Taylor & Francis, 1999).

4. Chess and Thomas, *Know Your Child*, 30.

5. Ibid., 32.

6. Howard Gardner, *Frames of Mind: The Theory of Multiple Intelligences* (New York: Basic Books, 1983).

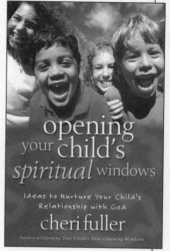

21 Days to Helping Your Child Learn

Cheri Fuller

Inside your child is a star student, excited about knowledge and discovery—and you can unlock that potential. How? By modeling your own joy of learning. Your excitement about learning can be infectious—and Cheri Fuller wants to help you help your kids catch the "learning bug"!

Whether your child is attending public, private, or home school, Cheri's insights will help you:

- Boost your child's curiosity
- Help your child study smarter
- Stimulate your child's creativity
- Impart optimism
- Use music to enhance your child's learning
- Expect excellence . . . and much more!

Following the plan outlined in this book, you'll see your child take more initiative in tasks, become a more active listener, and develop an ability to overcome obstacles. Best of all, you'll nurture the close, loving relationship with your child that makes learning an exciting, rewarding adventure.

Softcover 0-310-21748-2

ZONDERVAN™

GRAND RAPIDS, MICHIGAN 49530

www.zondervan.com